THE
HIDDEN
PEACE

FINDING TRUE SECURITY, STRENGTH, AND CONFIDENCE THROUGH HUMILITY

JOEL MUDDAMALLE

W Publishing Group

An Imprint of Thomas Nelson

Published in Nashville, Tennessee, by W Publishing, an imprint of Thomas Nelson.

Thomas Nelson titles may be purchased in bulk for educational, business, fundraising, or sales promotional use. For information, please email SpecialMarkets@ThomasNelson.com.

ISBN 978-1-4003-3534-3 (audiobook)
ISBN 978-1-4003-3533-6 (eBook)
ISBN 978-1-4003-3532-9 (softcover)

Library of Congress Control Number: 2023941250

Printed in the United States of America
23 24 25 26 27 LBC 5 4 3 2 1

To Britt,
This book would not have been possible without you.
Thank you for always keeping me rooted in truth.
Loved you first.

TABLE OF CONTENTS

CONTENTS

FOREWORD

THE HOLY LAND is so special to me. Every time I land and walk through the Tel Aviv airport, I whisper, "My soul is at home." This land that has seen so many changes through thousands of years has profoundly changed me.

One of my favorite stops is in Bethlehem. Some people don't like all the commercialism there. I get that. But if you ever go, please visit the Church of the Nativity.

This ancient church was built and rebuilt over the place where it is believed Mary gave birth to Jesus. If you were to visit this site today, you'd enter the church through a small door called the Door of Humility. As you approach the door marking the entrance, you'll see that it's much smaller than a standard door. In order to step inside, you have to bend your body low as you pass through the doorway.

As I entered this sacred space for the first time, I was struck by this thought: *God wants us on our faces before him, and there are two different pathways to get there.*

People who choose the pathway of humility before God choose to bow low out of reverence, honor, and dependence.

Others choose the path of humiliation instead. One ends up on their face before the Lord by *choosing* to bow low, while the other trips and falls there. Either way, both eventually end up on their faces before the Lord.

James 4:10 says, "Humble yourselves before the Lord, and he will lift you up" (NIV).

So I shouldn't be afraid of lowering myself in humility. But I should be aware of how pride can sneak in and cause us to fall in humiliation.

You might be hesitant to pick up and read a book on the topic of humility. *I get it.* Humility is often one of those topics we set high on a shelf thinking we'll address it *one* day, but it doesn't feel urgent for today.

Friend, can I lean in close and whisper something I've learned? *Today is that day.*

It's better to embrace and face our need for humility right here, right now, than to be knocked down in humiliation after a major fall or disastrous choice that echoes throughout all areas of our lives, the lives of the people around us, and the legacy we'll leave behind.

When it comes to talking and learning about humility, I believe Dr. Joel Muddamalle is the right person to walk with us through this conversation. Joel is a dear friend of mine, and together we have logged thousands of study and research hours on many different topics from Scripture. His humble approach to theology is refreshing to me, and I always learn so much from him.

I believe *The Hidden Peace* will not only encourage you deeply but will help you see your life and God's ways in a whole new light.

If you fear being outed, misunderstood, or wrecked if you take steps in this direction, you're in good company. It can feel so scary. Humility is never bought at a cheap price. It will always cost us something, but it will be worth the price we pay. I'm learning that humility not only costs us something; it also comes with a payout in the form of peace.

Peace. It's what we're all after, isn't it? Peace in our hearts and minds, in our homes, in the work we do, and in our relationships. As you work your way through the pages of this book, I pray that your heart (and mine) will be able to experience true peace from Jesus when we allow humility to shape our thoughts and decisions.

I want that so much.

I'm praying that you and I will see how God isn't trying to break our hearts or control us but rather make us ready for what he sees just ahead. Humility breeds peace, and peace creates a heart at rest.

Much love from me to you, friend.

—LYSA TERKEURST

INTRODUCTION

I'VE ALWAYS FELT a little out of place, as if I lived in two different worlds. I was born in the great city of Chicago and watched Michael Jordan soar in the air, wondering if he was ever going to come down. There was a Chicago deep-dish pizza spot around every corner and a Portillo's, with Chicago-style hot dogs, five minutes from my house. If you know, you know. If you don't, I'm sorry.

But though I was born in Chicago and was later raised there, I lived in India from the ages of two to five. Yep, I'm Indian. Like, from the country of India, home of the best bread you've ever had—garlic naan.

My parents left India in their early twenties to come to America. My mom was finishing her nursing degree and my dad was working night shifts as an X-ray technician. While my parents worked hard to create a strong foundation for their new life in America, they sent me to live with my grandparents in India. They trusted my grandparents and my mom's three sisters and two brothers to raise me an ocean away from them. I can't imagine how hard that was for my parents, but this is what good parents do, right?

They sacrifice for their kids. And my parents have a long history of sacrificing for their children.

So during those early years of my life, I ate Indian food, spoke Telugu (a major dialect of India), and lived my best life running the streets of a village called Jangaon outside the city of Hyderabad. It was in this little village that I experienced true safety, security, and stability.

My grandfather, K. M. John, was the headmaster of a prestigious local high school (and later, college). Everyone in the town knew him and, therefore, knew me. I would regularly go with him to work, sit in classrooms, and watch him teach. I knew exactly who I was and where I fit in life. I was the grandson of K. M. John, and my place was wherever he was.

Then, everything changed.

My parents were ready for me to come back to Chicago. So five-year-old Joey (that's what my family calls me) went back to America. I wish I could say that my return to the States was like the Eddie Murphy movie *Coming to America*—a prince of a foreign country stepping foot in America with the red carpet rolled out for him. But nah, that wasn't it. I quickly learned that I was no prince in this strange new land.

The first thing that struck me was how cold it was in Chicago compared to the warmth of Jangaon. The second thing I noticed was that I didn't look like the majority of the people; my skin was much darker. The third thing I realized was the food was different, and everyone used these weird things called forks, spoons, and knives to eat really bland food. In India we used our hands to eat, and the food was spicy—anything but boring. These three things—the weather, the people, and the culture—started to shake my sense of safety, security, and stability.

This was only the beginning of a thorough destabilization.

One of the first things my parents did to transition me into my new life in America was enroll me in a private Christian school. I expected this, of all places, to be where I'd feel the most comfortable. I mean, in India I'd basically lived in schools and watched my grandfather teach students, so this school thing would come naturally to me, right?

It turned out to be more complicated than I'd expected.

Coming right from India, my native language was Telugu. While I could understand English and speak a few words of it, I wasn't fluent. On the first day of class, I followed a crowd of kids walking into the classroom, feeling anxious since it was all so different from Indian schools. In the corner of the room, a bunny sat in a plastic cage, staring at us as we filed in. Corny posters hung on the walls, hinting at our coming adventures in learning.

Kids started finding seats. I didn't know where I was supposed to sit until I saw four familiar letters, *J-o-e-l*, on a name tag on a desk at the front. Relieved, I made my way to it and felt a surge of confidence, ready to dazzle my teacher and all the students with my brilliance.

The teacher started the day with an icebreaker and asked everyone if they had a pet.

I knew this answer! Without even thinking about it, I raised my hand and said heartily, "Dog."

Life would have been awesome if the conversation had ended here, but it didn't. She had a follow-up question (I hate follow-up questions). "Do you have a pet dog?"

"Yes, *dog*," I responded, with continued conviction, mingled with a bit of creeping fear.

Then came another follow-up question: "So what is your dog's name?"

I froze. My English vocabulary was pretty much at its end. I started to panic. With fabricated confidence I repeated, "DOG!"

Every kid in that classroom laughed. Not a little chuckle but a deep belly laugh. The teacher giggled. I think even the class pet, that weird bunny in the plastic cage who never stopped staring at me, was laughing at me.

There was one person who wasn't adding to the roar, and that was me.

The rest of that day is a bit of a blur in my memory, but my mom says I came home crying and yelling, "I want to go back home to India, to Jangaon!" I wanted to go back to safety, security, and stability, where I knew my place and everyone else knew me.

That classroom moment is my first memory of being truly hurt. I don't mean just "hurt feelings," like when someone didn't share a toy, or the pain from falling off a bike. This was a different kind of hurt. The kind that slowly makes its way deep into your soul. The kind of pain that makes you angry, then sad, then confused and frustrated, then angry again. It's a feeling that burrows to the core of your being over time, a type of deep-seated pain that actually begins to change who you are. Decades later, I can still remember the shame I felt when everyone was laughing at me in that classroom—that's how profound the impact was.

This change-who-you-are hurt left me with intense fears. It made me realize for the first time that the world was not a safe place.

What did I do with this information? How did I react?

I vowed that I would never let someone put me down or make fun of me again. I promised myself that I would always be the smartest person to walk into any room. And if I wasn't the smartest person, I would walk right out and never go back. I swore to myself that before someone could begin to make fun of me, I'd be witty and cunning enough to flip the script and turn the joke onto them.

I hated the feeling of being embarrassed and belittled so much that, according to my mom, I became fluent in English and lost my accent within just four weeks. While languages did come pretty easily to me as a kid, I worked *hard* at this. I was willing to do whatever it took to live an "unhurt life."

Maybe you can pinpoint your own version of this memory—the first time you realized the world didn't feel safe, when you were deeply hurt, when that pain created an even deeper fear of being hurt again. You also could probably name multiple times you've felt this way throughout your life—when pain absolutely gutted you and you had to live with the weight of new vulnerabilities and fears.

I'm pretty sure fear plagues most people in the world, but few of us will acknowledge it. And, as we're insisting, "Oh, I'm fine," the fear and hurt we're living with is robbing us of peace.

So, before you start saying that fear is not that big of a deal for you, hang with me for a second. What if you made a decision not to dismiss fear so easily? What do you think would happen?

I think if we can be brave enough to admit it's there and look closely at it, we can start to understand it. And if we can understand it and what has caused it, we can actually do something about how it compromises peace in our lives.

The fears we carry can look lots of different ways:

- fear of being exposed
- fear of being caught off guard
- fear of being let down
- fear of looking foolish
- fear of being hurt
- fear of being vulnerable
- fear of failure
- fear of danger
- fear of emotional reactions

- fear of being found out (examples: *I'm not a good parent. I'm a horrible Christian. I'm not good at my job.*)
- fear of being wrong
- fear of being rejected

I think if we were brutally honest with ourselves, we'd see that we are utterly controlled by some of these fears.

You might have the same reaction to identifying fears as I did years ago. I thought I had to get to a place in my life where nothing could hurt me. I wanted to figure out how to live "unhurt"—to avoid every fear and eliminate every weakness so nothing could touch me—so I'd feel safe enough to have peace.

If only, right?

This mindset is both a human instinct and a hopeless pursuit God never meant for us. As I learned what the Bible says about weakness and the pain that comes along with life, I realized that God never leads us to seek invincibility—it isn't even realistic.

And if we stubbornly resist reality, we'll live in a constant state of frustration. Our approach to finding lasting peace will never work. This is why we have to face reality: we aren't invincible, and we never will be. We all have fears that can lead us to experience hurt or to cause hurt in others.

God knows this.

And he has a way out for us.

He says to us now what he said to the apostle Paul: "My grace is sufficient for you, for my power is made perfect in weakness" (2 Corinthians 12:9 ESV).

This is vitally important for us. Here's why: it lets us know that experiencing peace isn't about dismissing fear, denying weaknesses, or avoiding pain. It's about acknowledging our fears and weaknesses and processing our pain in a way that redeems and brings meaning to all the hard stuff we've endured. Doing this brings internal peace, which then flows out to our external lives.

We will never be able to reverse our hurtful experiences. But we can redirect all our hurt toward the God who brings beauty out of ashes and let him lead us on a journey of experiencing his ultimate good for our lives.

Is this how our culture tells us to step into a good life? Not even close. We get a barrage of messages more like this:

- If I pursue (human) strength, I can cover up my weakness.
- If I gain (human) power, I can overcome my feelings of insecurity.
- If I achieve a sense of control, I can stop my life from falling apart.

In other words, if we can just win, no matter the cost, we will find the peace we've been longing for.

It's self-reliance, denial of weakness, and pretention all the way. And it never, ever works.

That's why we so desperately need the peace Scripture leads us into, even if the path it takes us on is surprising. It all begins with *owning* our lack of security, strength, and confidence. It's the exact opposite of self-reliance. This is what it takes to develop a God-given assurance that we can handle heartache—because we've thoroughly embraced dependence on him.

It all begins with *humility*.

The lost practice of humility is how you move toward strength, security, and stability. It is the means to the hidden peace you've been longing for.

You may have heard the saying "Humility isn't thinking less of yourself; it's thinking of yourself less." This is true, but I don't think it's complete. As I've studied humility in the Bible, I've found there are three parts to it: rightly understanding God, ourselves, and others. And the order matters. It doesn't start with focusing on ourselves; it starts with focusing on God.

Here's my definition: Humility is an awareness of who God is, which defines who we are and allows us to rightly relate to other people. It generates a settled steadiness in our soul and a capacity for fulfilling relationships. It gives us what we need to courageously move through every hard place in life and develop every godly virtue.

Humility. I know, it's unexpected. It's overlooked. It's undervalued. And that's exactly why it's so crucial that we retrieve this essential biblical discipline today.

I promise, you don't have to be a "super Christian" to read a book about humility. My friend and mentor Lysa TerKeurst often says, "Imperfect progress is still progress." And this is what I want to invite you into. Are you curious about how to deal with your problems in a way that lasts? Willing to take an honest look at your struggles? Open to hearing about God's way of living with peace, strength, and courage?

Then this is for you.

Let's go see how God is reaching out to us, inviting us into the good life, the peaceful life, that was always meant for us.

—JOEL MUDDAMALLE

PART I

LIVING THE FRUSTRATED, FEARFUL LIFE

CHAPTER 1

MISSING: PEACE, MY MIND, ETCETERA

"IT'S NOT FAIR! Why would they do that?"

"Kids are so mean!"

"We should have done more."

My sons, ages eleven, nine, and seven, stormed into the house and threw off their backpacks, grumbling and huffing and puffing.

"What happened? Why are you so angry?" I asked them.

All three boys started talking at once, and I could make out only a few words—*school, kids, playground, disability, jerks,* and *we hate them.*

After slowing them down and having them take turns, I heard about how kids at school had been making fun of a kid who had autism. As one of the boys finished the story, tears were streaming down the faces of the other two. They were really sad and incredibly angry, and they wanted things to be different. Finally, Lukey, the youngest, yelled out, "Kids suck!"

I was a bit in shock, but my instant reaction was, "Well, you're kind of right."

I'll pause to give you a little context here. Years ago when my wife, Britt, and I were dating, we both worked with people who had disabilities. She worked with kids on the autism spectrum; I worked with adults with dual diagnoses. When we started a family, we prioritized having our kids become familiar with this community. Since my boys had often played with kids on the autism spectrum, they understood the various support systems some of them need in terms of sound or light sensitivity.

Unfortunately, many kids aren't aware of this kind of thing, and when they encounter it, some of them freak out. Fear makes us do all kinds of terrible things. Apparently, the kids at the boys' school were afraid of what they didn't know, and they dealt with their fear by making fun of this kid on the spectrum.

> OUR GOD OF KINDNESS, COMPASSION, AND JUSTICE EXPECTS HUMANS, WHO HE MADE IN HIS LIKENESS AND IMAGE, TO DISPLAY HIS ATTRIBUTES.

My boys stepped in and stopped them.

"I'm so proud of you for doing that," I said. Then I talked about *why* it was right they did it, saying our God of kindness, compassion, and justice expects humans, who he made in his likeness and image, to display his attributes. That we need to recognize the image of God in others and treat them with respect and dignity. And that we have a responsibility to protect and defend people because we do life with God. Like Micah 6:8 tells us, "He has shown you, O mortal, what is good. And what does the LORD require of you? To act justly and to love mercy and to walk humbly with your God" (NIV).

OUR DYSFUNCTION, OUR CHAOS, OUR PAIN

I often think back to Lukey yelling out, "Kids suck!" and in my mind respond, *Yeah, but it's not just kids. Honestly, humans suck!*

I know I'm a theologian and I'm probably not supposed to say or write that, but y'all, I'm just going to be honest with you. In fact, let me say right here at the outset that I'm committed to honesty at all costs.

Sometimes, I feel like we are horrible humans. I feel this when I see

- grown adults trolling each other in the comments section of social media;
- a spouse acting out of selfishness and bringing chaos into their family because of their unloving, unwise actions;
- a friend ghosting another friend, leaving them wondering what happened to the friendship and if it was ever real in the first place; or
- someone shaming another person because of their personal belief or decision.

I sit back and simply wonder, *Why can't we just be better humans?*

I think it's because we were created with innate humility in our hearts, so if we lose humility, we actually lose part of God's design for humanity. When we live in a way that is inconsistent with how God designed us to live (humble), there is an incongruity between who we are and who we are meant to be. In other words, we struggle to live out what God intended for us.

> IF WE LOSE HUMILITY, WE ACTUALLY LOSE PART OF GOD'S DESIGN FOR HUMANITY.

God created humanity in his image, which gives us intrinsic worth and value. If everyone has this great worth and value, we should treat all humans—as image bearers of God—with honor, respect, and dignity. But y'all . . . are we doing that? And if not, why?

God also created us so we could know him. I think one of the reasons we suck as humans is that, at some point, we've lost sight of God. If we can't see God as he truly is, it is impossible for us to see ourselves as we should. This means we will think either too highly of ourselves (pride) or too lowly of ourselves (shame).

Here's the problem with both outcomes. If we think too highly of ourselves, we'll view every relationship through the lens of opportunity. We'll see every person as a pawn on a chessboard for us to move around and even sacrifice for our own benefit. When we receive praise, we will fall into an addictive cycle of desiring it and trying to absorb it until it eventually crushes us. We were never designed to absorb the praise of others; we were designed to pour out praise onto God, the only one worthy of praise.

If we think too lowly of ourselves, we will open the door for everyone to walk all over us. Ultimately, we will feel like we don't have a voice and, even worse, don't deserve one.

The longer this goes on, the more we will be robbed of peace. We will never be satisfied in our relationships because we will always be trying to figure out what else we can get from people. Or we will always feel dejected in our friendships because we've come to believe our lot in life is to be the one who sacrifices. The friend who always gives and never receives.

We may end up feeling totally insecure because we are always wondering if people are talking about us.

We may feel like we don't matter to the people closest to us and our needs will always come in last, creating a painful sense of our own insignificance in the world.

We may end up feeling like a failure of a friend because we keep getting abandoned by the people we opened up to and were vulnerable with.

We can even end up feeling guilty for having the beliefs and convictions we do if others look down on us or flat-out cancel us from a conversation.

The result is more anxiety, more fear, more pain, and more confusion than ever before. And this isn't isolated to just you and me. It is a societal issue that transcends age groups and demographics. In a Pew Research Center study, 41 percent of adults ages eighteen and older reported having "high levels of psychological distress" associated with anxiety and loneliness.[1] Barna Group found that 39 percent of adults they surveyed often felt sad or depressed. Another 34 percent said they felt isolated from others.[2]

I don't know about you, but nothing here sounds peaceful.

WHAT ARE YOU MISSING MOST?

So here's the deal. Go ahead and put a little check mark next to each line that reflects something you want:

- ☐ peace in your life
- ☐ healthy, authentic relationships with friends and family
- ☐ to not walk over other people
- ☐ people not walking over you
- ☐ confidence to face your fears
- ☐ courage to walk through your hurts
- ☐ an overall pattern of flourishing

If you put a check mark next to even one of these, you need to rediscover something that was an essential part of the Christian life for the early church but over time has slowly faded into an afterthought. We need to reclaim the lost practice of humility.

Right now feels like that awkward moment in a group discussion after a leader poses a question and it's totally silent. Everyone

WE NEED TO RECLAIM
THE LOST PRACTICE
OF HUMILITY.

is wondering, *Should I speak up? Is it me?* And as soon as you're ready to speak up, someone else jumps in. (Honestly, it's kind of miraculous how this seems to always happen.)

So let me go ahead and push us through the awkward and be the first to speak up.

Friends, this is my public admission. In the words of Taylor Swift, "It's me, hi."[3] I confess, I have a problem with humility because it terrifies me. I've run away from humility because I don't want to lose (human) control, strength, or power in my life. But the thing is, I've tried really hard to gain and keep all those things, and all it has done for me is make me more afraid of failure.

I spent many years in school and in theological training so I could add a few letters after my name. *If I can achieve a high level of education, I will be able to put my vocation in my own hands and guide it myself,* I thought. *I will earn a position of control, strength, and power.*

It turned out, though, that the more I studied and learned and "achieved," the more I realized what I didn't know. The more aware I was of my *weaknesses*. Those little letters I had longed to place after my name for so long transformed from symbols of victory into symbols of my secret internal insecurity.

Maybe for you it was a dream job you thought would put you on the path to success. But along the way you realized that the dream job was actually just a job and the dream was actually a nightmare.

Or maybe it was something as simple as having the security of a savings fund for a rainy day. Then the rain came and turned into a tornado that wiped out your savings and then some. The hope and confidence you once had was replaced with anxiety and uncertainty.

One way or another, you and I have tried to take things into our own hands and, in so doing, we've viewed humility as unwanted and unnecessary.

Yet amid all our angst and fear and opposition to humility, *it is actually humility that will move us forward*, into the life we're longing for.

OKAY, BUT FOR REAL . . . HUMILITY?

Now, you may be shaking your head, thinking humility is a threat that will squash your strengths and potential. I want to show you that it's actually a gift that helps the best of who we are flourish. You may think it will leave you unstable and weak. I want to show you it will actually make you steady and strong.

If you need more convincing, I totally understand. I did too. This is why I spent over a thousand hours studying humility in the Bible. At the end of my research, this is what I wrote in my journal.

What I've learned about humility and why it's actually worth pursuing:

Humility refuses to allow us to think too highly of ourselves.

Humility rejects a low and degrading view of ourselves.

Humility reorients our view so we see ourselves as God does.

Humility looks at the success of our brothers and sisters and encourages us to celebrate them and not be threatened by them.

Humility helps us see the value of our work but won't let us define our worth by what we do.

Humility gives us the courage to face our failures and learn and grow from them.

Humility guards our hearts from the seduction of personal success so we aren't crushed by the praise of humanity.

Humility continually reminds us that we were created to reflect God's glory, not to try to absorb glory for ourselves.

I need humility because, honestly, I've tried everything else, and none of it has worked. I've still felt anxiety about the reality of my weakness. I still fear being walked on and over. If you're in the same spot or something like it, welcome. Hi, it's me. It's nice to meet you.

CHAPTER 2

FROM PANIC TO HONESTY TO REST

I WAS BACK in Chicago at last. And it was better than ever because I got to share it with my wife and kids.

Since high school, I'd lived in Joplin (Missouri), Naperville (Illinois), Sacramento (California), and Bellingham (Washington) for school and work. After five brutal years of living in Bellingham, where I traveled over a hundred thousand miles a year for my job, my family and I had the opportunity to relocate to Chicago. The area had it all—amazing food, historic sports teams, a massive airport, and, best of all, a supportive community.

At the time, my wife, Britt, and I had three boys under the age of seven. Liam was five, Levi was three, and Luke was eleven months old. Today we have a fourth child, Emelia Jane, who the boys fight over to tickle and hug.

One thing you need to know about our family is we have nicknames for everyone. We call Brittany *Britt* or *Britty*. My close friends and family call me *Joey*. We call Liam *Bubba*. Levi's nickname is *Leviathan* or *Bebi* (pronounced *bee-bye*). Luke has a bunch of nicknames—*Lukey, Tookey, Lucario, Lukey Bear*—but we almost always refer to him as *Lukey*. We call Emelia Jane *Emmy, Em, EmJ* (which is my fave—if you know, you know), or *The Notorious EmJ*.

Once our family of five was in Chicago, we loved that we could jump in the van for a three-hour drive to Indianapolis, where my parents lived, for a long weekend. After years of not seeing my mom on her birthday, we decided we would drive down and surprise her. There was no greater gift for my mom than to spend her birthday with her grandsons!

We were hitting the road after dinnertime so the kids could sleep in the car, and as I loaded up the van, eleven-month-old Lukey was a little whinier than usual. He hadn't slept well the night before, so I chalked it up to cranky tiredness. As Britt put him in the car seat, she mentioned that he felt a little warm. But babies often run a little warm, so we took note and carried on.

Soon Lukey became extra fussy and kept trying to raise his hands around his seat straps. We assumed he was frustrated about being in the car and would work himself into a sleep soon enough.

After about an hour into the ride, he finally fell asleep while the two older boys were quietly watching a show on our iPad. We felt like we were crushing it as parents. We played my friends Shane & Shane's *Psalms, Vol. 2* album—starting with the song I was obsessed with, "Psalm 46," then putting it on repeat until Britt eventually got annoyed and made me shuffle all the songs. Before long we would surprise my mom, earning me the trifecta award of best son of the year, best father of the year, and best husband of the year.

Fifteen minutes from my mom's house, Lukey started crying. His cries quickly ramped up to shrieks of pain. A concerned Britt looked at me, then back at the car seat.

Then Lukey made one more extreme scream and went silent. Without hesitation, Britt unbuckled and jumped back to his seat.

Everything in my mind slowed down and sped up at the same time. It felt like the whole world was spinning.

"Joel, pull over right now and call 911!" Britt yelled. "Lukey is limp! He's not responding to me!"

When I heard those words and the quiver in Britt's voice, fear struck me. It attempted to paralyze me. But I managed to park the van and called 911, saying my eleven-month-old son was nonresponsive and we needed help as soon as possible. I didn't even know the street we were on; I just told them which highway exit we'd taken and that we were in a steak house parking lot.

"Stay calm," the operator said. "Help is coming."

Stay calm? Impossible. I was petrified.

In a split second every worst-case scenario bombarded my mind. Was he breathing? Was he brain damaged? How could I possibly fix this? Hands shaking, legs wobbling, I rushed out of my seat and opened the van's side door. There was my precious boy, his big brown eyes half-open, staring off toward the left.

I feverishly unbuckled him, swooped him up in my arms, and found myself screaming, "Lukey, Lukey! Wake up!" over and over and over. Still nothing. Half of his body convulsed and jerked almost mechanically; the other half was limp and motionless.

As my panic hit a fever pitch, everything else became a blur. I faintly heard my two older sons crying, "What's wrong with Lukey?" And I caught glimpses of Britt in shock, mouth open, tears streaming, then whispering, "We need help . . . Someone help us . . . We need help."

THE LORD OF HOSTS IS HERE

I was at the end of myself. I had started this trip with a sense of security and stability. But here in this moment, holding my baby boy, I started to plead with God in my spirit to be our help—to send rescuers and to be present in our moment of helplessness.

A deep-seated fear started to whisper in my heart, telling me how useless I was. How incapable I was. All the control I thought I had as a parent, as an adult, had fallen apart in a moment after a single scream. All the strength I possessed could not shake life back into this child's body that lay still in my hands. And any power I had could not force the paramedics to appear in an instant.

In this single moment of pain, I came face-to-face with the reality of my inability. I was forced, by circumstance, into honesty. It may have been the most humbling moment of my entire life.

Then, a single phrase from the song I'd been listening to ("Psalm 46") reverberated in my heart: *The Lord of Hosts is with you.*

At this point, I was more terrified than ever, but I clung to this simple sentence in response to the fear. An answer to its accusations. The next step in my posture of honesty. The fear was still there, but so was an indescribable peace.

It's hard to describe what took place in the next moments; it was a raw and intimate conversation with God within my heart that went something like this.

God, I can't control what's happening right now. I feel like everything is falling apart, and there's nothing I can do about it.

God: The Lord of Hosts is with you.

God, every ounce of strength I thought I had has been depleted. I'm weak and panicked. I don't know how I can do this.

God: The Lord of Hosts is with you.

God, I feel powerless and empty. Everyone is looking to me to do something, but I'm completely at a loss!

God: The Lord of Hosts is with you.

God, I believe you. You're here. You can handle this.

In those panic moments, the primary thing my heart needed to be reminded of was the eternal truth of God's nearness to me.

The unshakable reality of the presence of God within me. This anthem of truth, "The Lord of Hosts is with me," led me to face the crippling fear and pain.

It turned out I needed the reality of God's presence even more in the moments that followed—when the paramedics arrived, took Lukey away from Britt and me, and carried him into an ambulance. I remember losing sight of Lukey's little body as he entered that ambulance. Not being able to see him anymore reinforced the overwhelming feeling of *I just can't do anything. I can't fix this or help him. And if I can't, who can?*

This is where God met me.

After a few minutes they waved us over, and we saw Lukey moving, coming out of what looked like a deep slumber. The paramedics informed us that he had been crying in pain because he had a double ear infection. This had caused a fever, which had spiked and resulted in a febrile seizure. Apparently, this is common among children; it's a way the body resets itself when it's overheated. The paramedics doubled him up on ibuprofen and Tylenol in order to relieve the pain from the ear infection and reduce his fever.

Lukey received care at a hospital for a few days, and then, to our relief, he was fine and came back home with us.

Our life did change from that point on, though. We had to start checking his temperature at the first sign of sickness. If he was at or above 99.9, we gave him ibuprofen and Tylenol and cooled him down with a lukewarm washcloth on his forehead. Lukey hated that part the most, so we called the washcloth his "Batman," because, of course, it turned him into a superhero.

Even with all these precautions over the next few years, Lukey had more febrile seizures. But by the time he was five, he grew out of them.

Throughout those years of seizures, fear was a constant for us. If we got even a hint of Lukey being sick, our hearts would beat faster as we rushed to check and address his symptoms. To this day, whenever he has a fever, we feel fear. We're triggered by the pain of that first seizure, and, if we aren't careful, it can send us into a tailspin.

THE RELENTLESSNESS OF FEAR AND PAIN

The memory of past pain can creep up on us from unexpected places and create whiplash, leaving us sore for days, months, even years. As you read these words right now, you may feel the pain of that whiplash creeping up on you, and I know how that feels. It hurts. And we just want it to stop.

How do we stop the pain and prevent the triggers? How do we protect ourselves from fear?

Our culture offers a few answers: Achieve control, show strength, gain power. Fight and scratch your way toward them, hack them, find a cheat code, fake them; however you can, pursue them at any cost.

Here's the problem though: the human versions of these are all illusions. They look real, they seem promising, but ultimately they are false—that is, as long as we're trying to conjure them up on our own. In the next few chapters, we'll look closely at each of these pseudo-antidotes and why they cannot help us relinquish our fears or pain.

I want to pause here and acknowledge that these things are not exclusively bad or wrong. If we have *zero* control, strength, and power, we find ourselves in a frightening place. Like next to an ambulance with our convulsing child. For years, Britt, Liam, Levi, and I felt that same helplessness and fear overwhelm us whenever Lukey suddenly had a seizure, and I became desperate for a way out of those feelings for all of us. I wanted to gain some level of control, strength, and power to prevent us from experiencing those emotions. But whenever I grasped for the "Joel versions" of control, strength, and power, I inevitably came up short, which only multiplied my frustration and stress.

SOMEONE BIGGER CHANGES THE GAME

Let's go back to Psalm 46 and look at the promise of God that changes the conversation—something we can hold on to when we are presented with false promises of the world: in the midst of our deepest fear or the most horrific disaster, "*the LORD of hosts is with us*" (vv. 7, 11 ESV).

"Lord of hosts" is a militaristic Hebrew phrase used here to refer to God as the King of the heavenly army. But there is a huge difference between the type of King our God is and the kings of this world. The kings of this world often stay back in hiding during war, distant from the conflict. They wield control, strength, and power from a position of safety, far behind the armies they send into battle. God, however, is the type of King who is on the front line of battle. He alone wields ultimate strength; all power flows from him. The King is in control.

The promise of Psalm 46 is the presence of the King in the midst of our fear—the King who personally walks us through our pain. We have a Battle Leader. He will meet us in our panic moments, our living nightmares, and bring his power into the picture.

All eleven verses of Psalm 46 can encourage our fearful hearts as they assure us that God is in total control over all things. The psalmist broke it up into three categories: God is in control over nature (vv. 1–3), over our enemies (vv. 4–7), and over the entire world that is in war and chaos (vv. 8–11).

> WE HAVE A BATTLE LEADER. HE WILL MEET US IN OUR PANIC MOMENTS, OUR LIVING NIGHTMARES, AND BRING HIS POWER INTO THE PICTURE.

As we begin to grasp the absolute ability of God, we see its contrast with our inability. And if we humbly accept our limits, we can gladly rest in his vastness. We can move from fear into peace, into assured faith in the Lord of Hosts.

Now, there's a key word in this foundational concept. Did you catch it? *Humbly.* This is the turning point of managing fear differently in our hearts.

Humility is what flows out of humanity when we

1. see God as he truly is,
2. see ourselves in light of who God is, and
3. see others as God does.

Cultivating humility also helps us see every situation and circumstance as something God rules over and can bring good out of.

This is what Psalm 46 invites us to—a greater awareness of God, which directly impacts how we view ourselves, others, and our circumstances.

Let's take a closer look at how the psalmist proved that we can face our fears with confidence. Verse 2 says:

> Therefore we will not fear though the earth
> gives way,
> though the mountains be moved into the heart of
> the sea. (ESV)

The psalmist used imagery of seas and mountains, two symbols that held specific meaning for the ancient Israelites. The mountains were places of stability and security. They were unshakable and unmovable. The sea, however, was an image of disaster and chaos. It brought destruction. What a frightful scene it would have been if the safe, strong mountains were swallowed up by the ravaging sea!

In contrast to this, verses 4 and 5 tell us that God carries his people not into the chaos of the sea but to the peace of the river: "There is a river whose streams delight the city of God" (v. 4 BSB). While the mountains, the very things that seem unmovable, might be thrown into the sea, God can never be moved; and this unmovable, unshakable, peace-bringing God will be our help "when morning dawns" (v. 5 BSB).

I love this. Each dawn of a new day is a reminder of the help we have in God. Every morning when the sun rises, the overwhelming strength of God is put on display. He is the God who "breaks the bow and shatters the spear; he burns the chariots with fire" (Psalm 46:9 ESV).

Now, at first glance, we may overlook the battle language used here and why it's so impressive. Part of the challenge we have as readers of the Bible in the twenty-first century is that we are far removed from the historical, social, and cultural context of the Ancient Near East of the Old Testament. If we weren't, we'd know that the bow and spear were considered some of the deadliest weapons at the time.

> EACH DAWN OF A NEW DAY IS A REMINDER OF THE HELP WE HAVE IN GOD.

An expert archer could shoot a bow from a distance with extreme accuracy. An archer started his training as a child and practiced until he had the ability to pull a bowstring under a hundred pounds of pressure and shoot an arrow a distance between three hundred to four hundred yards.[1] While the bow and arrow were lethal distance weapons, the spear was a lethal mid- to close-range weapon. The lighter version of a spear (javelin) could be thrown at midrange distance, and the heavier spear was used in close-range combat.

The final military reference in Psalm 46:9 is a chariot.[2] While the word *chariot* appears in the English Standard Version of the

Bible, the Hebrew word indicates something more like a "war wagon," a vehicle used to deliver military supplies and carry the treasures or spoils of war back home.

If you were faced with archers or spearmen on a battlefield, you'd be in for a tough fight, but it'd still be winnable. If you saw a war wagon, though, it would change the entire makeup of the battle. When you and your enemy inevitably ran out of ammunition and other supplies, the war wagon would deliver a load of essentials to your enemy with impressive speed. Bringing a war wagon to a battlefield would be like bringing a gun to a knife fight. Absolutely unfair and, for the outmatched opponent, totally terrifying.

What did God do in response to these lethal military weapons? Well, he broke the bow, he shattered the spear, and he burned up the chariot with fire (v. 9). He shut it all down, showing his might and proving himself to be greater than every human battle. I love that last description of burning the chariot with fire. In ancient times, this act of destroying weapons was seen as "a token of peace, and wars being caused to cease, there being no more use for them."³ God was ushering in peace.

What does this tell us about God? Whatever you and I fear that is far out in the distance or up close in front of us can be overcome by the Lord of Hosts, who is with us. And, if the scariest thing we could even imagine, like a war wagon, shows up in our battle, whether it's a diagnosis we never saw coming or a relationship we couldn't imagine being without, God will be with us to help us move through or overcome even that. He is always able to usher in peace.

MARVEL AT WHAT HE CAN DO

What a humbling yet empowering invitation we have to "come, behold the works of the LORD" (Psalm 46:8 ESV) that we may ultimately be reminded of the truth that "the LORD of hosts is with us; the God of Jacob is our fortress" (v. 11 ESV).

Psalm 46 shows us that, while we may not be able to avoid fear or stop hurt in our lives, we are promised the nearness of God to help us face our fears and get through our hurt. Psalm 46 helps us see ourselves honestly so we can rightly see the majesty of the Lord of Hosts. This leaves us in a posture of humility as we become more aware of what we are unable to do and as we marvel at all that God continually does on our behalf and for his glory.

> WHILE WE MAY NOT BE ABLE TO AVOID FEAR OR STOP HURT IN OUR LIVES, WE ARE PROMISED THE NEARNESS OF GOD TO HELP US FACE OUR FEARS AND GET THROUGH OUR HURT.

So, just as we are invited to see the works of God in Psalm 46, I want to invite you to come and see how God alone can grant us the peace we long and hope for. But before we can get into that, we need some honest exploration. In the same way I was forced into honest awareness of how little I could control in that parking lot, we need that level of honesty to explore the depths of our hearts.

Now, I won't be forcing you into anything. I'll lovingly encourage you to join me in the exploration. To be honest, things may get difficult as we face longings of our hearts that need reorientation. But all of this, I promise you, is good. It's what I've needed and continue to need. Typically, in order to get to the good, we need to go through some hard.

So, friend, let's keep working through this together, remembering the promise of Psalm 46 along the way: "The LORD of hosts is with us; the God of Jacob is our fortress" (v. 7 ESV).

If you are in the midst of a situation that feels impossible, or in a moment of longing for hope and help, you have a promise from God—one of the most significant promises he could give.

He is with you!

Friend, tuck this little truth away into your heart. The promises of God are rooted in the character of God. God's character is trustworthy and true. If he says he will be with you, you can have confident assurance that he will keep that promise. Why? Because that's just who he is—a promise keeper. And if he is with you, it really doesn't matter who lines up against you, because he who is in you is much greater and more superior than anything this world will try to throw at you (1 John 4:4).

PART 2
FIGHTING TO MAKE
"MY WAY" WORK

CHAPTER 3

"I CAN'T KEEP IT ALL TOGETHER": HUMAN CONTROL

I'M GOING TO let you in on a little secret that is totally embarrassing. But after sharing the hardest and scariest moment in my life to date with you, I think we've built enough trust to continue on our trajectory of honesty.

As a kid, I had a really hard time falling asleep. Actually, I still struggle with it. Whenever I try to wind down from the day, my mind wanders and shoots off in wild directions, and it won't let up, like a hamster relentlessly running on its wheel. Usually the only way I can manage to get it in shut-down mode is to exercise my imagination.

This is where things get a little embarrassing.

When I was young I loved the idea of camping, having a dog, and going on an epic survival journey. But my family was not a camping family. We were barely a stay-at-a-hotel family. So the only option I had was to imagine such an adventure.

I used to lie in bed at night and picture myself camping by a glowing, crackling fire and feeling a chilly gust of wind that created a tension between the warmth of the fire and the cold of the night. I would imagine I had a pet dog that was fiercely loyal and protective and would stick close by me, ever attentive. Naturally, his name was Dog. (*The Walking Dead*, anyone? Daryl is my fave.[1]) The night sky was clear with all the stars shining bright, the type of brightness that can't truly be treasured with the disruptive artificial light of houses and streetlights. It was a brightness that was natural, untainted, and piercing as it lit up the night sky. Somewhere in the middle of imagining all these details, my mind would wander off to sleep. I did this pretty much every night throughout my childhood. And . . . yeah, sometimes I still do it as an adult. And by "sometimes" I mean "kind of often." Okay, now do you see why I said *embarrassing*?! I don't love admitting this, but, hey, you have to find what works for you, right?

Over the years, I often wondered why this childhood practice was so important to me—and so effective. It has almost always given me a feeling of calm assurance and stability. Eventually I realized that I grew attached to this exercise because it provided a sense of control. It was a moment when I picked my situation, down to the last detail. Beforehand, my mind had been trying to manage and resolve a bunch of things from throughout the day—all from my limited kid world, sure, but each of them a reminder of my lack of control.

So, any chance you have your own version of this nighttime mental wrestling?

Maybe at night you carry out your bedtime routine—teeth brushing, face cleansing, pimple patching, lights dimming. You put on cozy pajamas and crawl into bed, ready to stick to the smart boundaries of reading a book—not getting engrossed in your phone—before lights out. On the way to pick up your book, though, your phone flickers with a notification.

What if it's important?

Pause, deliberate.

I'll just check the preview message on the screen to be safe.

An hour later you are deep in emails, Facebook comments, Instagram reels, and the newest TikTok fads. You notice the time and panic—you stayed up way later than you meant to, given your early morning. You scramble to disconnect your mind from the Facebook argument you've been debating whether to "like," save the IG reel to share with your "close friends" later, and finally set down your phone.

Lights out. Covers up. Comfy sleep position.

Eyes closed.

Now, deep sleep. *Go.*

In the quiet, the questions that have been lurking in your subconscious hit you. Will your boss give you the project you can't stand? Will your kid keep talking back to you tomorrow—and will she ever grow out of it? What if the heartburn isn't just heartburn? Will your ill father get better after chemo? What if he forgets to take his pills? Will the car give you trouble in the morning?

As your mind races with all the things you have no control over, you toss and turn and eventually drift off, only to wake up every hour, anxious that you overslept—then toss and turn again, battling your thoughts more. After a maddeningly restless night, the alarm goes off and you force yourself up, feeling overwhelmingly sluggish and disoriented as you start another day.

After hours of obsessing over what you cannot control, you feel, in a way, even more out of control.

"YOU'VE GOT THIS" DOES NOT APPLY

Many of us experience this regularly; the struggle is real, y'all. Lacking control has got to be one of the most disturbing, unsettling feelings we can have. For this discussion, let's define *control* as the ability to personally exercise power, strength, and authority over situations or people to get an outcome we desire.

It feels like if we could just gain more control over our finances, relationships, work, and academic careers, we'd be freed from the fear of the rug being pulled out from under us. We'd feel safer. It seems like control is the missing piece to the stability and peace we long for, right?

Not quite. Gaining and wielding human control in order to establish stability is an alluring promise—but an empty one. Though it might seem like we can reach it and it will work, we'll eventually see it's a deceitful illusion. Everything we thought we were in control of was actually out of control.

I've yet to come across a single person who can guarantee absolute financial security or honestly say they're in total control over any relationship in their life. I personally know loads of people who achieved the peak of academic success and later suddenly found themselves jobless. But I don't know anyone whose academic journey played out perfectly, ending with the ideal degree and career.

As an active Instagrammer and as the director of theology and research at Proverbs 31 Ministries, I regularly receive messages from women who've found their once-unshakable marriages in shambles. Sometimes their messages leave me absolutely sick to my stomach. One woman who had been happily married for more than twenty years found a massive amount of money missing from her savings account. As she dug in to find answers, one discovery of deceit led to another. Her husband had spent her money on pornography and illegal, destructive substances. She felt betrayed and heartbroken, and wondered if any of the happiness she'd shared with him all those years was ever real or just an illusion of happiness.

Every year of my life, I become increasingly aware of how unable I am to truly control anything. Not long ago, Liam broke out in hives after playing in the woods, suffering a severe allergic reaction to poison oak. Immediately, Britt and I were like, *We've got this.* We gave him Benadryl and called a doctor . . . and then sat by helplessly as the hives spread all over his body. When his eyes started to swell, the doctor said, "I recommend going to the emergency room. This could be the

EVERY YEAR OF MY LIFE, I BECOME INCREASINGLY AWARE OF HOW UNABLE I AM TO TRULY CONTROL ANYTHING.

beginning of anaphylactic shock." The general tone of *We've got this* quickly turned into utter panic and chaos as we rushed to the ER.

To our relief, he got a steroid shot, which kept the allergic reaction at bay. It then took more than a week of meds and topical ointment before his poor body finally cleared up. He was eventually fine, but in those early moments, Britt and I felt paralyzed in helplessness, unable to stop the swelling or remove the poison oak from his body.

This is just one example of how I regularly encounter my own inability and become intimately familiar with my weakness. Other times I see people who won't bend to what I want or think is best, and I can't control them. Whenever I realize this, I feel like I am out of control myself. And whenever I try to gain control, it's like I'm attempting to break down a concrete wall with my own brute force.

How do I end up feeling? Worn out and irritated. Bruised and beat down. Dissatisfied and tense. Exhausted and unable to find peace.

Not unlike how I feel after a sleepless night.

SOMEONE'S ALREADY GOT THIS

When we come face-to-face with this reality, we have two options. One, we can freak out, thinking the whole world is truly falling apart and there is nothing we can do about it. I want to be honest with you; this response is totally understandable. But I want to suggest that we can also move from this to another response.

Two, we can exercise faith. We can take a deep breath. Lift our eyes to the sky and watch the clouds still in place, the sun still shining, and recognize that oxygen is still present with each breath of air. As we pause, we can be reminded that our lack of control in fact reveals to us the one who is in control. What we see confirms and informs our faith in the invisible one who created all things.

The Old Testament prophet Nehemiah said it this way: "You, LORD, are the only God. You created the heavens, the highest heavens with all their stars, the earth and all that is on it, the seas and all that is in them. You give life to all of them, and all the stars of heaven worship you" (Nehemiah 9:6).

Maybe the most practical thing we can do when we feel a loss of control is gaze at the stars, remind ourselves of the waves of the ocean, and marvel at the one who created it all. As we take a minute to just focus on the wonders of God, we could whisper to ourselves, "And I didn't have to do a thing."

We don't have the weight of responsibility to keep the stars in their place, a great reminder as we're falling asleep! We don't carry the burden of ensuring every living animal in the sea is cared for. The Lord, the God of heaven and earth, is taking care of the entire universe because he is the only one truly in control.

> THE LORD, THE GOD OF HEAVEN AND EARTH, IS TAKING CARE OF THE ENTIRE UNIVERSE BECAUSE HE IS THE ONLY ONE TRULY IN CONTROL.

Friend, if this is true of creation, what does it mean for the jewel of all creation—humanity?

It means God is intimately involved in our lives. He is aware and never caught off guard by anything we face.

REACH OUT AND FIND HIM

The apostle Paul gave us some assuring words to cling to when we feel like things are out of control. He spoke them when he was on Mars Hill, a place where philosophers and people would gather to ask deep questions. "What is the meaning of life?" someone might ask, or "Why is there evil in the world?" Each of those questions has an underlying root: an awareness of our inability to control everything we want to.

In Acts 17:24 Paul echoed what the prophet Nehemiah said. God made the world and everything in it, and he didn't need any help! Then, Paul went on to make a life-changing, perspective-shifting statement: "From one man he has made every nationality to live over the whole earth and has determined their appointed times and the boundaries of where they live" (v. 26).

Okay, so sometimes I am guilty of reading the Bible way too fast. I want us to slow down and really take in what Paul was saying here.

1. "From one man he has made every nationality to live over the whole earth."

   Who created the first humans? God did, and we know from Genesis 1:26 that he created them in his likeness and image. Here Paul explained more, saying that all of humankind, including every nationality and culture, finds its origin in God, and they live over all the earth because of God.

2. "[God] has determined their appointed times and the boundaries of where they live."

   We could be tempted to think that God created everything, then stepped back and left it to run its course. Paul refuted that idea, giving two aspects of God being in control. First, he determined our "appointed times," and, second, even the "boundaries" of our existence are determined by God.

Why is this so crucial in helping our fear of losing control? Because it reminds us that there is not an ounce of our human life that is random or by chance. Think of it this way: you and I could have lived in any point of human history, yet we live now. There is a purpose to why we live in this specific moment in history. We could be located in any geographical location, yet we live in the country, state, city, neighborhood, street we do for a reason! It's not random. It's not out of control. It is ordered and has a purpose.

So what's that purpose? Paul said, "He did this so that they might seek God, and perhaps they might reach out and find him, though he is not far from each one of us" (Acts 17:27).

If we take a closer look at the original language Paul used here, we'll see he actually acknowledged our loss of control. The phrase "they might reach out" translates from the Greek verb *psēlaphē-seian*, which can also mean "to look for something in uncertain fashion, *to feel around for.*"[2] The word is used elsewhere in the Bible as well as in ancient Greek literature to describe a person who is either blind or stuck in darkness and trying to find or "feel" their way out of their dark and desperate situation—a situation in which they are painfully aware of their need and their lack of control.[3]

> IT'S A HUMBLING EXPERIENCE TO BE LOST. BUT THAT NEWFOUND HUMILITY PAVES THE WAY FOR IMMENSE GRATITUDE AND JOY ONCE WE'RE FOUND.

Paul said that while we are in this situation, searching for escape, for some kind of guiding help, God is near to us. And as we reach out and seek him, we will find him and realize that he has actually never been far.

So, the situation we're in is not good. Things are looking dire, and panic is settling in. But if we'll stop and look up, we'll find the security and peace of our God who assures us that we've never been alone. He's been there the whole time, and he will continue to be with us.

It's a humbling experience to be lost. But that newfound humility paves the way for immense gratitude and joy once we're found.

We're going to come back to this connection between humility and leaning on God's control, but I want to close this chapter by suggesting something that may feel a little scary. What if our lack of control—even when it leads to anxious nighttime thoughts, moments of panic, and desperate attempts to gain control—is actually a gracious gift of God? What if it sets us up to realize that the very belief that we can control things is really an illusion? As soon as we can identify it as an illusion, we are positioned in a posture of humility and recognize the one who is truly in control of all things. Then we are straight shook when we look to our side and realize he's been with us the whole time.

In Hebrews 11 we read, "By faith we understand that the universe was created by the word of God, so that what is seen was made from things that are not visible" (v. 3). God, in his might, did the unimaginable, creating the entire world we live in today. He is the one behind the strength and beauty we see all around us. He is also the one at work in every detail of our lives. And it's by faith that we understand all this.

So when we confront the reality of our lack of control, it's an opportunity. We can exchange our desire for control for the gift of humble faith.

We can stop spinning our wheels. Stop wearing ourselves out with fruitless

> WHEN WE CONFRONT THE REALITY OF OUR LACK OF CONTROL, IT'S AN OPPORTUNITY. WE CAN EXCHANGE OUR DESIRE FOR CONTROL FOR THE GIFT OF HUMBLE FAITH.

efforts and ratcheting up our inner tension. We can begin to experience a deep, settled peace in our souls by accepting the reality of our lack of control and embracing Jesus, who has perfect control.

As you lie awake at night, sleepless and restless, consider speaking some simple truths over yourself as a prayer.

Jesus, you are with me.

Jesus, I can't, but you can.

Jesus, you are my peace that brings calm.

Now, let's take a breath. Think of his awesome power. And let ourselves just *accept reality*, that so much of life is not in our hands. And that's okay; it's in his.

CHAPTER 4

"I HAVE TO WIN AT ALL COSTS": HUMAN STRENGTH

IF YOU EVER ask me to play the card game Speed, my instant reaction, without even a thought, will be an emphatic no.

It's not that I dislike games—I love them. If you ask anyone who does life with me, they will tell you I am a very competitive person. But I have a hard time playing games that magnify an area of ineptitude for me.

I first played Speed when I was dating Britt. She quickly realized I was competitive, and I could tell she didn't have a competitive bone in her body. At least that's what I thought.

Britt's family taught me how to play their favorite family card game, Hand and Foot. It's one of those all-day-long type of games. Take a break for food, then get back to it. The learning curve was steep, but, boy, did I love beating them at that game.

On one of our Hand and Foot–game days, Britt innocently asked me, "Hey, do you want to play a quick game of Speed?" I had never played it, but I was kind of tired of winning so often at Hand and Foot, so I figured, *Why not liven up my winning streak with a new game?*

Britt sat down with a quiet confidence and explained the rules of the game. I thought, *This is easy.* Then, for the next forty-five minutes, I lost. Not a single win. I never even got close to winning. It was one of the most humbling moments of my game-playing career!

Britt and I have been married now for thirteen years and together for fifteen. I attempted to beat her at Speed in our first few years together but never could. Then I stopped playing it altogether. Why? Because I'm afraid to lose! There, I said it. (*Yes,* I'm admitting this in a book about humility . . . I did promise honesty!)

ANYTHING BUT A LOSS, PLEASE

Losing is the worst. Why is it so miserable? Why do we run from it? Why would we do whatever we can to prevent it?

Well, I've come to realize that losing exposes our weakness.

It surfaces through all kinds of losses in our lives. In my example with the game of Speed, it was a type of intellectual loss, but there are so many more:

- physical loss
- emotional loss
- financial loss
- relational loss
- material loss

Any type of loss forces us to face our weakness, and weakness is detested in our culture. It is associated with inability or failure, and it's often connected to the poor, powerless, or outcasts of society. This is why our culture begs us to avoid our weakness and over-emphasize our might, superiority, and strength. In this discussion, we'll define *strength* as our ability to accomplish what we set our minds to by our own physical, emotional, or mental fortitude that reinforces a belief in our self-sufficiency.

The other day I was filming an episode in a Proverbs 31 Ministries podcast series called *Therapy & Theology*. While my fellow cohosts and I were getting prepped, which includes makeup for all of us, one of them looked at me and said, "Uh, Joel, you have a serious white hair in your beard." I was shook.

Then, someone else commented, "Actually, he has several in his beard and some on the side of his head."

At this point I was sweating. Was this something good? Was it bad? Should I be embarrassed or just laugh it off?

"Do you guys want me to pull them out?" I asked.

They all emphatically said no and started laughing.

For my friends, the white hair was just an observation. For me, it was evidence of my mortality and ultimately my weakness. My white hair was a visible symbol to the world that weakness was no longer just coming for me; it had arrived.

I swear, as soon as this happened, I started seeing ads for Rogaine on Instagram and noticing hair color products at Target. Same story for commercials during Monday Night Football. The media was hounding me about changing my hair, pushing me to try to convince everyone I was younger.

We've got to ask, why all this messaging about covering up, removing, or preventing white hair on our heads? Why the huge investment in product lines and promotional media? The resistance to aging in our culture—and throughout centuries of cultures—is so extreme. (Remember those ancient stories about people trying to find the Fountain of Youth? Yeah, this ain't new.) *Why?*

Because the white hair is a visual representation of our limitations and weakness. We are finite and we are aging, and we don't like *not* having the power to change those realities. So if there's anything we can do to distance ourselves from those realities—like getting rid of white hair—we will do it in order to feel further from our limitations and weakness.

Teresa of Ávila, a prominent Christian thinker of the 1500s, spoke to these issues, and I think she was onto something so important:

> Let us not trouble about our fears nor lose heart at the sight of our frailty, but strive to fortify our humility and be clearly convinced of how little we can do for ourselves, for without the grace of God we are nothing. Let us confide in His mercy and distrust our own strength in every way, because reliance on this is the root of all our weakness.[1]

Teresa wisely pointed out fear and frailty as sources of our trouble, as reasons why we work so hard to cover up, avoid, or fix our weaknesses. It's likely that fear influences our desires and dictates our thoughts and actions more than we'd guess.

Just the other day, my own fear reared its ugly head as I posted on social media. Ah, Instagram, where we get to be super selective about what we post; where we can so easily shift from healthy connection to unhealthy comparison; where so many of us share only our best, most flattering bits of life and feel shrunk by looking at everyone else's.

My fear-monster moment began as I was taking videos of my eleven-year-old son in one of his flag football games. Liam threw an amazing red zone dart and scored a touchdown. I caught it on video and posted it on my IG.

Next, he let a deep ball loose and let it float in the air. It was a great throw, but it got picked off. I caught it on video—but I did *not* post it.

On the next drive he had an amazing rollout to his right and threw a perfect pass to his wide receiver on a crossing route that resulted in a seventy-yard touchdown. I posted it. You never would've known there was an interception between the two touchdown passes unless you were at the game.

On the drive home my wife asked innocently (which is always an indicator that it's a loaded question), "So, babe, why didn't you post that interception?"

I instantly responded with the best excuses I could think of. Oh, I wasn't really thinking about that. It was a quick post. The interception video was a little longer. I didn't want to hurt Liam's feelings by posting that video.

And finally, with that last response, I got closer to the truth.

The honest truth was, in my heart I didn't want the social media world to have a vision of my son as weak. An interception was an indication of weakness. I wanted everyone to see Liam at his strongest moments.

But it gets worse.

I was also afraid people would think, *What is his dad doing? Don't they practice?* My own insecurity was a major influence in what I posted. I was concerned about being viewed as deficient in some way.

I eventually admitted this to my wife and processed it all with her.

Later that week, Liam and I were looking at the game film (something we always do to help him improve), and we came across that clip of the interception. I took a moment to remind Liam that his value and worth didn't come from how well he did something. His value and worth were also not diminished by him doing something wrong or not incredibly well.

And I had to also remind *myself* that others' perceptions of me don't determine my true identity. No exposed weakness or perceived weakness could ever change my true God-given value and worth. The same goes for any appearance of strength or any true achievement. My identity and value are fixed and settled, apart from any of that, by God. And when I forget that, when I go without that settled assurance down deep in me? I fall into insecurity *real fast*.

As author John Dickson wrote, "The more you rely on achievement for a sense of worth, the more crushing every small failure will seem. It is analogous to the fashion model who depends on her beauty for a sense of personal value; every blemish is a disaster, and she lives with the reality that her beauty is sure to fade. . . . High achievers of every kind are setting themselves up for insecurity if they pin their sense of self-worth on their accomplishments."[2]

DEPENDENCE ON THE KING

I am the firstborn in my family, which means that, when I was growing up, I carried a lot of responsibility. This may be a universal firstborn thing, but it feels, to me, especially true in Indian culture. Not only am I the firstborn son, I am the firstborn grandson in my extended family on my mom's side, which only amplified the pressure I felt. Everything I did was supposed to be an example for my siblings and my cousins. Even if you're not a firstborn, you probably know about the constant weight of these kinds of expectations and how crushing they can be—especially when you make a mistake, and it seems like the whole world has its eyes on you. Feeling like your personal worth is constantly being evaluated, and like you're sometimes deemed "not enough," can send you into a tailspin.

You may have grown up in a family situation that demanded a lot from you.

You may have bought into a vision of the good life that was totally dependent on your strength and perfection.

You may now live with the crippling burden of each mistake reminding you of your weakness.

You may wonder, *Is there another way?*

There is. The great theologian J. I. Packer wrote, "Weakness is the way."[3] It's the way for us to come to terms with our limits. It reminds us of what we can do and what we can't do. The reality of weakness lets us off the hook of expectations of perfection. In a way, weakness is the prerequisite to God giving us help. As Scripture tells us, "While we were still *weak*, at the right time Christ died for the ungodly" (Romans 5:6 ESV).

If no one else says this to you, I want to say it to you:

You are not defined by your successes.

You are not defined by your failures.

Your value and worth come intrinsically from being made in the image and likeness of God.

Look at how Genesis 1 describes the origin of humanity: "God said, 'Let us make man in our image, according to our likeness. They will rule the fish of the sea, the birds of the sky, the livestock, the whole earth, and the creatures that crawl on the earth.' So God created man in his own image; he created him in the image of God; he created them male and female" (vv. 26–27).

> YOUR VALUE AND WORTH COME INTRINSICALLY FROM BEING MADE IN THE IMAGE AND LIKENESS OF GOD.

The first thing we learn about the nature of humans is that God created them in his image and likeness.

An often-overlooked aspect of humanity is the position of vulnerability and weakness they are in. They are created beings; they require the breath of life that comes from God alone. Their first natural state was one of vulnerability and weakness—but that was totally okay, because they were fully reliant on God. God met their every need and desire.

Two Hebrew words are used in reference to the creation of humans in these verses from Genesis: *tṣelem* is translated as "image" and *demuth* is translated "likeness." These words are connected to royalty and divinity. In the Ancient Near Eastern world, specifically in Mesopotamia and Egypt, they were used to describe human royalty and their relationship to the divine.[4] Given this linguistic context, Genesis 1 is presenting Adam and Eve "as king and queen of creation," as the children of the great King of all creation, Yahweh.[5]

Just a curious question here: What did Adam and Eve do to deserve the breath of life and the power, position, and authority of being called children of the King? Search Genesis 1 and 2, and you'll get a clear answer: *nothing*. Again, God simply bestowed on them what they needed—and more.

Prior to sin entering and corrupting the world, weakness was not something to be despised. It was beautiful evidence of dependence on God. Vulnerability was not something to fear. Dependence created intimacy, which was vital for enjoying the unique relationship between God and humans.

> BEFORE THE FALL OF HUMANKIND, WEAKNESS AND VULNERABILITY WERE NOT THINGS TO DESPISE OR FEAR BUT THE NECESSITIES FOR LIVING IN COMMUNION WITH GOD!

Let's really hold on to this idea. Before the fall of humankind, weakness and vulnerability were not things to despise or fear but the necessities for living in communion with God! After sin entered the world, weakness and vulnerability became tools of the Enemy to create chaos and division in human relationships, both with one another and with God.

What we need to lead us out of this chaos is the very thing creation needed to bring order to its chaos: light.

STARE DOWN YOUR WEAKNESS
TO GET TO STRENGTH

Let's jump back to when God made the world. When it was just darkness covering the earth, "God said, 'Let there be light,' and there was light" (Genesis 1:3). The light was "good," and God separated the light from the darkness (v. 4).

Light exposes the darkness. Light brings clarity and vision. Light illuminates what is hidden. Light eases the anxiety of the unknown.

The light God brings into our lives exposes our weakness and vulnerability. It's the reality God wants to reveal to us (for the purpose of developing further dependence on him), and we typically *do not want to see it.* But, boy, are we missing out. Because the more you and I grow in dependence on him, the closer we get to returning to the Eden-like existence that God first intended for Adam and Eve.

Confession: I'm not a morning person. It's a tragic confession for a theologian. When I study the greatest theological and biblical scholars, I always find that they were morning people. I don't get it, but it is what it is.

Lysa TerKeurst and I were once guests on Levi and Jennie Lusko's podcast. During our conversation I shared that I was working on becoming a morning person. This was, unfortunately, nothing new for me; it's been a lifelong pursuit I've perpetually fallen short in.

I admitted to them that when I do manage to get up early in the morning, I tend to be a mean morning person. If someone wakes me up by yanking open the curtains and abruptly letting light blaze onto my face, things will get ugly. I'll feel like I've been shocked into existence, and it's painful. Granted, after a little while, my eyes will adjust to the light, and, before long, mean morning me will be replaced with normal me.

And after that podcast recording, you know what those kind friends Levi and Jennie sent me as a gift? An alarm clock that simulates the light of the sun, gradually increasing until it hits full intensity at the alarm time. It's still disruptive (I still don't like getting out of bed), but comparatively, it's a more pleasant way to wake up.

We have two options when it comes to facing our weakness, and they coincide with these two ways of waking. We can try to shut out the light, desperate to keep it from revealing our vulnerabilities, resistant to the idea of depending on God. We might manage to hide from it for a while, but eventually the light will burst into our space, making our weakness abundantly clear. And it will be just as disturbing and painful as sunlight exploding into our bedroom, jolting us awake, leaving us disoriented from the shock.

Our other option is to allow the light to gradually increase and continually work in our lives, little by little every day. We can welcome the light because we trust it will be good to us and for us. And if we can keep reminding ourselves why the light is good, we will be able to tolerate the difficulty it brings.

Either way, we don't get to choose the light. The light that shines on our vulnerability will come to us, whether or not we welcome it.

But if we open our hearts to welcome it, we will be positioning ourselves to move into new strength—God's strength. We'll be able to experience the stability that comes from embracing weakness as we live the life of Christ.

VULNERABILITY CONNECTS YOU TO THE SOURCE YOU NEED

I need you to hear something and let it really sink down into your soul.

Are you ready?

Your weakness is not a sign of being worthless.

Likewise, your strength is not an indication of your superiority or self-sufficiency.

God himself secures you in your identity and worth, apart from these issues of strength and weakness. And more than that, he meets you in your weakness and empowers you for the life he wants you to live.

St. Augustine of Hippo, a North African bishop from the end of the fourth century through the first third of the fifth century, said, "O Lord my God, Light of the blind and Strength of the weak, and at the same time, Light of those who see and Strength of those who are strong, listen to my soul and hear it crying out from the depths."[6]

God is the source of light for the blind and strength for the weak. God is also the source of light for those who see and of strength for those who are strong.

> GOD MEETS YOU IN YOUR WEAKNESS AND EMPOWERS YOU FOR THE LIFE HE WANTS YOU TO LIVE.

In other words, regardless of our specific context of weakness or strength, God is the source that provides, leads, and helps us. Why would we cut ourselves off from depending on him?

Our first parents, Adam and Eve, were in a position of weakness and vulnerability, just as we are today. For them, those things simply meant more dependence on God and intimacy with him. Are you willing to view your vulnerabilities through this lens? Are you willing to embrace weakness, knowing it will lead you to the source of all strength—Jesus?

To think about how this would look practically, let's use a sort of self-diagnostic assessment, remembering that God often uses the people in our lives to sanctify our souls. Honestly consider if you are willing to

- admit when you are wrong and thank the person who brought it to your attention;
- ask for feedback when you are uncertain about something and be genuinely open to what you receive;
- pray for the Holy Spirit to reveal areas of weakness that you are trying to cover up and present as strength;
- bring those weaknesses the Holy Spirit reveals to a trusted friend or mentor and process why they might be there (what other issues they might be connected to); and
- lay those weaknesses down at the feet of Jesus and say, *Lord, make this area of my life a soil for your presence to take root in. Use my weakness to bring more of your strength into my life.*

I had an opportunity to run through this self-diagnostic tool myself just the other day, when Britt and I were in an airport. Just the two of us were on a trip (a rarity with four littles in our house) to celebrate a friend's birthday. I am a frequent flier, so I have TSA PreCheck. Britt doesn't, but usually when I book tickets as a family, her ticket prints with TSA PreCheck. I assumed (first massive problem) that this would be the case for this trip.

When I travel, I like to get in and out as fast as possible. As I beelined to the TSA PreCheck line, Britt kept saying behind me, "Uh, babe . . . my boarding pass . . ."—but I didn't have time to hear all that.

When we reached an agent and she looked at our boarding passes, she said, "Sir, you have TSA PreCheck, but your wife doesn't."

I paused. Britt was staring at me. Then I said what I thought was the most reasonable and logical thing to say: "Babe, I'll head through PreCheck, and you can go through general screening. I'll meet you on the other side."

Britt continued staring at me for what seemed like eternity. She looked into my very soul. Then she simply said, "Excuse me?"

At this point I realized that I'd made a mistake. (After thirteen years of these fumbling, foolish moments, the signs have become clearer.) I walked it back and said, "Let's both go through the general security line." *The extremely long and inconvenient general security line where I have to take off my shoes and take out my electronics.*

"Sounds good," she replied.

We then waited in line in silence. She was upset with me. I was frustrated I had to wait in line.

Humility . . . it can be practiced anywhere, even in an airport.

Now for that self-assessment. Had I been wrong? *Yes.* Being together with my wife while we travel is more important than convenience. It took a few hours, but eventually I was able to process what had happened and get Britt's feedback on where I went wrong and how my decision made her feel. My thought process and actions showed that I cared more about my own personal preference than being with my wife and not leaving her alone! For her, the trip was about being together, having quality time. Moving quickly wasn't on her list of priorities.

We had a great (and hard) conversation that taught me that my pursuit of personal convenience led me to a lack of self-awareness and consideration of Britt. I was exercising pride, not humility. And this was a weakness that God wanted to shed light on within my heart so he could continue guiding me into actually living the life of Christ.

WEAKNESS PROVIDES AN AVENUE FOR US TO EXERCISE GOD-DEPENDENCE.

I left that conversation thinking that the weakness we experience is an actual kindness of God. Weakness in fact breaks the myth of self-reliance. Weakness provides an avenue for us to exercise God-dependence.

You may be smack in the middle of doing everything you can to cover up your weakness. You may be full steam ahead in doing your best to deny the reality of your inability. But friend, I want to suggest that, with only a fraction of that energy, you can simply accept the limits of your weakness and allow that to lead you into further safe dependence on God.

Be encouraged that your brave honesty—your willingness to accept the reality of your weakness and who God says you are—will not ultimately diminish you. It will actually produce humility, nudging you to lean more and more into Jesus' power, putting you on the path toward infinite strength.

So go ahead. Step into the freedom of saying, "I will boast all the more gladly about my weaknesses, so that Christ's power might rest on me" (2 Corinthians 12:9 NIV).

CHAPTER 5

"I'M NOT SURE I'VE GOT WHAT IT TAKES": HUMAN POWER

I THINK ONE of God's favorite ways to bring humility into our lives is through our kids.

I can honestly say there has never been a dull moment when it comes to my second son, Levi. He is smart, funny, and so rambunctious that, early on in his life, I started calling him my "Leviathan." A Leviathan was an ancient sea monster (think dragon in the sea). I'll let you sit with that image; it's proven true of my son over the years.

One day I pulled into our driveway after a long day at work, ready to see my family. The driveway was lined with large pine trees at least twenty feet tall. The higher you got, the tinier the tree limbs. On this particular day there was absolutely no wind. However, I noticed that one tree in the row of trees was swaying right to left. I thought it was curious but continued walking toward the house.

Then, all of a sudden, I heard a panicked voice screaming, "DAAAAAADDDDDD! HELP ME!"

I turned around and looked up to the sky, wondering why I was hearing Levi's voice coming from the heavens. I never thought God's voice would sound like Levi's. Then I realized the voice was coming from a little brown dot at the very top of one of those massive trees.

Yep, every parent knows the feeling. Panic followed by pure frustration and anger. But first, get the kid down safe.

So I guided Levi down from the tree, walked him into the house, and started very passionately explaining how irresponsible, dangerous, and flat-out dumb it was for him to climb that high into the tree. With each minute that passed, I got closer to his face to really get my point across. The closer I got to his face, the more his face crinkled and cringed from pain. I was getting through to him, and this would truly be a lesson learned for him.

Finally, after a good five to seven minutes, I asked, "Okay, now what did you learn?"

Levi looked at me with straight pain in his face. "Dad, did you brush your teeth this morning? Your breath stinks so bad!"

The Leviathan struck again.

There were a lot of things that could have gone through my mind in that moment. *How did this kid miss the point? Does he not realize how serious this is? What did I do wrong? Clearly, I wasn't angry enough!*

Instead, I thought, *Wait . . .* did *I brush my teeth this morning? Does my breath actually stink? How many people at work had to endure my hot breath today?*

My immediate posture was insecurity, which has plagued me for as long as I can remember. This bad breath remark from my kid was really no big deal, but it still triggered me. The deep insecurity I've had all my life came rushing to the surface.

GOD CAN WORK WITH THAT

I've always had this fearful thought running through my head: *I'm not that special.*

I was never the smartest kid in a classroom. To my parents' dismay, I wasn't the little Indian guy impressing the teachers or winning spelling bee championships.

I was never the most athletic kid. To my own dismay, as much as I wanted to "be like Mike," I was five foot eight and 175 pounds by the end of my high school career, the textbook example of "average."

I was never the super-spiritual kid in youth group. I wasn't winning the Bible sword drills or getting the "Bible bucks" for memorizing Scripture, and my heart didn't leap for joy at the thought of folding and packing up all the chairs in the sanctuary after youth group.

I was never the cool kid in high school. I desperately wanted to be cool; I wanted to fit in and sit at the popular kids' lunch table. I wanted the cool girls to like me—heck, to even acknowledge me. I wanted to get invited to the cool kids' parties, but my invite always seemed to get lost in the mail. I was just the Indian kid at Neuqua Valley High School who was kind of funny and had friends in different social groups.

The pattern continued into Bible college. Confession: in my first semester, I failed three of my five classes and was put on academic probation. (Can someone say *irony?*) I loved the Bible, but I wasn't the kid the best professors handpicked to disciple because I had the raw skills to become the next megachurch pastor. I longed for a sense of validation and significance, but I often felt overlooked.

But throughout these "I was never" aspects of my formative years, a sovereign God was working in my life in unexpected ways.

I realize now how fortunate it was for me that I was never the smartest person in the room, because it meant I was always learning and growing, constantly motivated by the awareness of what I was not but wanted to become.

I realize now how valuable it was that I didn't have superior natural athleticism, because it forced me to be a team player. I learned that we experience success as a team when we play together as a team.

I realize now how dangerous it is to be someone who considers themselves "super spiritual" and solely focused on winning Bible sword drills, because it can lead to an assumption that we can "win" at learning the Bible. I was protected from thinking that the study of Scripture can be something we can achieve, master, and move on from.

I realize now that God was working in me as a high school kid while I built friendships with people in the margins, learning to relate to many different kinds of people, because the family of God is made up of different kinds of people from different backgrounds, ethnicities, and cultural perspectives. In a way my social situation in high school trained me for my spiritual situation in the family of God, which is multiethnic, multicultural, and multigenerational.

And I realize now that pursuing achievement, notoriety, or popularity in the Christian world is a fast track to destruction that can often lead to utter humiliation.

So many "but I'm not" and "they are" situations run through our minds. You may be mentally rehearsing some of these scripts right now.

You may be thinking, *I'm not the smartest person in the room.*

I'm not the most creative person in my friend group.

I'm not the one who can create something beautiful from something ordinary.

I'm not the one who'd win a Parent of the Year award. (In fact, if I get just a Mother's Day or Father's Day card, I'll be good!)

For every one of these "I'm not" thoughts, I want to remind you of something—something I've desperately needed over the years and still need to this day.

I may not be . . . but God certainly is.

God is the smartest and most powerful one of all. He is the origination of creation, the one who can take the ordinary and turn it into something of magnificence.

Throughout these years of writing myself off as depressingly ordinary or weak, feeling achingly inadequate, God had a whole different perspective and agenda. God wanted to remind me of who he is smack in the middle of all that I am not. He used my insecurity to help me grasp how much I needed him, to steer me toward wisdom, and to form me into someone who wanted to operate in his power, not my own.

I can now look back at all my "I'm not" moments and see how God can truly work with my insufficiencies. And I am so convinced the same is true for you.

THE COST OF GAINING HUMAN POWER

As we're grappling with insecurity, feeling desperate to escape it, there's another big danger we need to be aware of. When our insecurity is met with fear, we might consider actions that will compromise our character.

Compromise often starts when we decide we'll do whatever it takes to gain power. Power deals with influence and authority. It presents itself in the way we dress, in our access to resources to get what we want, or in our confidence in our charisma or personality. We may have been told that the way to deal with insecurity is to place ourselves in positions of power. But what is the cost of gaining that power?

If there is one person in the New Testament who can attest to the cost of gaining and exercising power, it's Paul. His Jewish name was Saul, and he came from Tarsus. He had a privileged upbringing and Roman citizenship, which is where the name Paul came from.

Before Paul met Jesus, Paul was passionate about the Israelites being faithful in their relationship with God. He didn't want them to be coerced into a cultural allegiance with the world and deny the lordship of Yahweh. At that point for Paul, the only way to ensure this was a strict and total return to the Torah (or the Law).

He said, "I advanced in Judaism beyond many contemporaries among my people, because I was extremely zealous for the traditions of my ancestors. But when God, who from my mother's womb set me apart and called me by his grace, was pleased to reveal his Son in me" (Galatians 1:14–16).

In a position of great influence, Paul thought he was doing everything God wanted him to do. The problem was, in his zeal, Paul missed the person of Jesus. Paul was persistent in using his own power to force people into a relationship with God.

But consider this: God in Christ Jesus laid down his power through the incarnation as an invitation for humanity to exercise humility and follow him.

I love how New Testament scholar Timothy Gombis describes Paul's ambition and motivation: "Paul assumed that on the day that God saved Israel by pouring out resurrection, God would vindicate him on the basis of who he had become in the eyes of others. . . . He had equated the praise of men with the anticipated praise of God."[1]

How do we accept, or rationalize, the cost of acquiring power to protect us from deep-rooted insecurity? We justify our actions. Paul justified them because he equated his actions with the works of God.

How do you and I justify them? We tend to rationalize by

thinking, *Everyone makes small character compromises, and it works out in the end. It's no big deal.*

We may think that the end justifies the means. *Sure, people may question my character today, but tomorrow they are going to be glad I'm in a powerful position, because I can do so much more good!*

The problem is that the end does matter, and how we get there is just as important as getting there.

The challenge is that small character compromises are directly connected to major character flaws. Character flaws inevitably create relational and situational chaos that will eventually erode peace. Those flaws in our character can become the biggest problems in our lives—especially if we initially overlook them or write them off as insignificant.

YOUR POWER SOURCE IS KEY

You may be wondering if there is any hope at all for us to deal with our insecurities in a healthy way. There is, and you may be surprised to hear what it is. It's to pursue power. The kind of power that has been made available to us through Jesus—not the kind we attempt to gain for ourselves.

Later in Paul's life, after he started following Jesus, he said, "My goal is to know him and the *power* of his resurrection and the fellowship of his sufferings, being conformed to his death, assuming that I will somehow reach the resurrection from among the dead" (Philippians 3:10–11).

The power we need for addressing, going through, and overcoming our insecurities and fears is the power that comes from Jesus and his resurrection. Notice the specifics of how Paul described his goal. It was not to "gain the power of the resurrection"; it was to "know him and the power of his resurrection"!

We need to long for the right kind of power—the power of the cross of Jesus.

And the way to experience that power is to know Jesus.

Okay. *How* exactly do we know him?

This is where things get really interesting and, honestly, a little scary. I've said this before and I'll say it again to you: I'm committed to honesty at all costs, especially when it comes to the Bible. There are parts of Scripture I wish weren't there. It would make my life as a theologian so much easier. But I want us to be honest about the text because our honesty will lead us to humble understanding and personal fulfillment.

> WE NEED TO LONG FOR THE RIGHT KIND OF POWER—THE POWER OF THE CROSS OF JESUS.

Paul could have given us a long list of places in the Gospels we could learn about the power of Jesus and his resurrection. He could have said "through the miracles of Jesus." Or even "from the ascension of Jesus as he goes to sit at the right hand of the Father." I mean, I would even take "through Jesus' clever responses to the Pharisees and Sadducees every time they tried to corner him in a theological debate."

Instead, Paul referenced Jesus' own teaching about himself, saying the way we experience the resurrection power of Christ is by sharing in the suffering of Christ.

Let that settle in for a moment.

Suffering, frailty, weakness, insecurity, instability, feeling overwhelmed, coming to the very end of ourselves—these all, through the lens of Christ, are not to be despised but cherished. They are the very things that connect us to him and to the power we are desperate for. When this connection takes place, we experience peace.

It can feel overwhelming and honestly an unfair task for God to assign to us. It can feel like an act of cruelty to suggest that the way we can experience power, stability, and security is through suffering and weakness.

And this would be true if God did not give us a peculiar yet powerful gift. The gift of humility. A gift that has for too long been left unopened, discarded, and lost as we've tried to gain the benefits of the gift (security, strength, and confi-

> THE WAY WE EXPERIENCE THE RESURRECTION POWER OF CHRIST IS BY SHARING IN THE SUFFERING OF CHRIST.

dence) without cherishing and learning how to live Christ's humble life today.

PRACTICE BEING HONEST ABOUT YOUR LIMITS AND NEEDINESS

When I was about twelve or thirteen, I woke up in the middle of the night and headed to the kitchen to get a glass of water. I was surprised to find the lights on and my mom sitting at the kitchen island, visibly upset. She was staring at the phone, her eyes red, her lips quivering, her cheeks covered in tears. She seemed to be in a state of shock.

"Mom, what's wrong?" I asked. "Why are you awake so late? Who were you talking to?"

She looked back at me and paused, then told me the nightmarish truth: political radicals had kidnapped my grandfather from his home in the middle of the night. They had been threatening my grandfather for years—warning him to stop preaching and teaching about Jesus—and finally, all those threats came true that night.

A few days later, we got the full story. A group of men blindfolded my grandfather, tied him up, put him in the back of a Jeep, and drove him up a mountain. Once the vehicle reached the top, he heard the sounds of guns being loaded and cocked, ready to be used.

My grandfather's captors told him they wouldn't kill him if he would simply deny Jesus and agree to stop talking about him.

"I cannot do as you ask," my grandfather replied. "I will not deny Jesus. And how can I say I love him but never tell others about him? Do what you must."

He began to sing a worship song as he anticipated seeing Jesus in a few moments.

What happened next is wild. I can share only what my grandfather experienced. As he was still blindfolded and tied up, he heard his captors suddenly start screaming with terror. They dropped their guns and ran down that mountain as fast as they could.

Confused, my grandfather sat still and waited awhile. Eventually one of his captors came back to help him and led him back down the mountain. Still blindfolded, still tied up at his hands, my grandfather just kept singing songs about Jesus all the way down.

We later found out that the returning captor had been a student of my grandfather as a child. But, to this day, there are other parts of this story we can't explain. Was it a supernatural event where God intervened? Did an animal show up and scare those men? Whatever happened, it took place at my grandfather's most intimate moment of weakness, a point in his life when he simply had to accept the reality of his inability. And when he was vulnerable and pressed in the most intense way, his response was honest humility.

OUR RESPONSE IN MASSIVE MOMENTS IS THE CULMINATION OF THOUSANDS OF SMALL MOMENTS.

You may be reading this thinking, *Gosh, that's such a massive moment. How do you know how you'd respond in such an extreme situation?*

I think our response in massive moments like this is the culmination of thousands of small moments—whenever we have the
opportunity to practice humility. And so, every day, we want to
get our hearts positioned for this kind of response to vulnerability,
instability, and suffering. We want to practice being honest about
our weaknesses and where we reach the end of ourselves—however
we can, even in small moments—so we are in the habit of bringing
our neediness to the only one who can provide for all our needs.

In later chapters, we're going to dig into a biblical theology of
humility. The humble theology that Christ embodied and passed
on to his first disciples. The humble theology that was the driving force of security, strength, and confidence for the first-century
church as it endured immense persecution and pain. It's what Jesus
is calling us back to today. It's also what the Enemy of our souls is
hell-bent on distracting us from.

I'm just going to lay it out there for us: humility isn't sexy, and
that's probably why it doesn't "sell" today in our society. But I'm
convinced part of that is because it's been
a while since our culture has seen the quiet
power of biblical humility at work. I think
part of the reason is because there is a real
Enemy who wants to keep us away from the
power of God's gift of humility in our lives.

If humility is God's gift for us, we
need to be aware of how the Enemy tempts
us to reject it and tries to convince us that
it will leave us helpless. The temptation is
powerful and seductive. It is both visible
and unseen.

> IF HUMILITY IS GOD'S
> GIFT FOR US, WE NEED
> TO BE AWARE OF HOW
> THE ENEMY TEMPTS
> US TO REJECT IT AND
> TRIES TO CONVINCE
> US THAT IT WILL
> LEAVE US HELPLESS.

How exactly does the Enemy attempt to prevent us from living
the humble life?

Through pride.

CHAPTER 6

"MY HEART TELLS ME SO": HUMAN PRIDE

"CAN I HELP you, sir?" the Best Buy employee asked as I was comparing three different TVs.

"Sure, that'd be great. I'm looking to replace my old TV."

I shared with him a horror story of a boy, a football, and a sixty-five-inch TV. (Yes, it was as devastating as it sounds. And yes, there were some new hard-and-fast house rules after that one.) The employee and I had a mini therapy session as he consoled me. Then he started on his sales pitch for the best TV to replace the broken one.

I'm a questions guy, so I started firing them off. What's the resolution? What's the processing speed? Is it a smart TV? How does it do with video game consoles? After all that, it came down to clarity of picture, really only degrees of difference between the models. As I stood there, evaluating the picture disparity in minute pixels between two basically perfect screens, a flash of a memory hit me.

I was seven, and my dad had just brought home a new TV

that promised twelve channels. It was twenty-two inches with an antenna even bigger than the screen.

"Joey, go move the antenna! We need a better picture," my dad said.

I moved the antenna around. "Better yet?"

When the antenna was in a bad location, the entire picture was distorted. Streaks of gray, black, and a few random colors spilled across the screen with only momentary flickers of a clear picture. The distortion was maddening.

And here I was years later, looking at a picture in such high definition that I could make out every little detail. I had full awareness and vision.

Now, if a football crashed into it, like one had tragically crashed into my previous TV (I'll always remember the good times we had), that perfect display would be distorted. What once was clear would become unclear. I'd be left guessing what I was looking at. But you and I don't have to live in that state of disorder.

> THE POWER OF HUMILITY IS THE CLARITY IT BRINGS US.

The power of humility is the clarity it brings us. It allows us to see ourselves and others the way we ought to. When we see ourselves the right way, we're more secure and confident. We feel more joy and satisfaction. When we see people the right way, we can treat them well and build healthier relationships.

But there's something that often stands in the way between us and this clarity, between us and humility.

Pride.

Pride hijacks our ability to be self-aware. It distorts our view and interpretation of things.

Have you ever been in a conversation with someone who is not in tune with his listeners' disinterest in the topic at hand? This unaware guy assumes everyone is hanging on his every word—it's all fascinating, pure gold. He reads their expressions as saying, *This is riveting!* and *How is this guy so brilliant and charming?* when in reality they mean, *How the heck do we get out of this conversation?* and *Please get on with it so we can politely step away and retreat to the other side of the room.*

In time, the guy with no self-awareness will see a pattern; every time he starts talking, the group around him slowly dissipates. A lack of self-awareness will turn into a spotlight of unwanted awareness that just hurts.

It hurts when we realize people are actually not interested, when people walk away annoyed, when we're seen as unimpressive.

And none of us want to hurt.

When have you been on the receiving end of a lack of self-awareness?

Maybe when you talk with your friend about something deeply personal, they change the subject and totally overlook your vulnerability. It hurts.

Maybe you share honestly with your spouse how the home dynamic (with the kids, work, all the things) is wearing you out. You can't keep running at this pace, and things need to change. They respond only with, "Yeah, I get that. Let's for sure focus on this." And then nothing changes in the slightest. It hurts.

Maybe your friends know you're in a financially tight spot, but they still make plans to go to a restaurant way outside your budget, never considering what it will do to your feelings. It hurts.

Where can we trace this hurt back to? Pride. It prevents people from being self-aware and derails you from being aware of others, which leads everyone into trouble. People do it with us, and, yes, we do it with others.

Last summer, a group of my childhood friends visited our family in North Carolina, and I took them on a hike up Crowders Mountain. The higher we went, the more aware we were of how small we were and how large that mountain was. We grew to value and cherish the rails and safeguards that were built into the mountain as we ascended to the peak.

Once we reached the top, the view was stunning. I couldn't help but think of people saying, "I feel like I'm on top of the world." But I also realized how deceitful that view could be.

Standing on that mountain, we felt like we were in total control and completely safe and secure. But the thing is, if we'd gotten too far over that ledge, one slip would've turned that beautiful view into a frightening fall, causing bodily injury or even death. Standing on that mountain safely required self-awareness, wisdom, and an acceptance of our limits. Lacking any one of these things could be fatal.

When we act in ways that lack self-awareness and are rooted in pride, it's like we're playing recklessly on a cliff with no concern for what could happen to us or others.

Thomas à Kempis, a late-medieval-period author, theologian, and monk, said, "Proud people do not truly know themselves, nor do they perceive their own calling, condition, and destiny clearly."[1]

Pride clouds our vision. So as we walk up the mountain of life, we need to consider not only who we are but *whose* we are. We have to rely on God to give us a full vision of ourselves (the way he sees us), so we don't end up on a cliff unaware and acting in unwise ways.

> AS WE WALK UP THE MOUNTAIN OF LIFE, WE NEED TO CONSIDER NOT ONLY WHO WE ARE BUT *WHOSE* WE ARE.

HEADS-UP: WHAT'S AT THE
ROOT REALLY MATTERS

Now, you may be thinking, *Oof, tough time for proud people. I'm so glad that's not an issue for me.*

That may be true. But let me gently suggest that there is an overt kind of pride as well as a *hidden* kind of pride. Hidden pride may be the most dangerous and vicious because you don't recognize it in yourself. Others may not either. Hidden pride can even initially present itself as the fruit of the Spirit like being kind, good, gentle, and humble—but at the root, there is a sickness.

One year at IF:Gathering, an incredible women's conference run by my friend Jennie Allen, I met author Ann Voskamp, who quickly became a new friend. (If you've read Jennie's or Ann's books, I just want to confirm for you that they are the real deal.) Ann told me she was excited about her plan to bring a lamb onstage for a session at IF. I was like, "Hold up—a lamb? Like a real-life lamb?" Ann assured me I'd heard her correctly.

The next morning I watched Ann walk that stage with a lamb and then interview a real-life shepherd named Darryl. I found their conversation fascinating.

"What dangers do you fear most for your sheep?" Ann asked him.

"Well, there are two kinds of dangers," Darryl explained. "Visible and invisible. The visible threats are the coyotes and other things in the environment. The invisible threats are parasites that can invade the stomach lining of the sheep and cause serious damage over time. At first, the sheep will look totally fine. They look like sheep, smell like sheep, and walk like sheep."

On cue, the baby sheep in Ann's arms gave the cutest *baa* you ever heard.

"But growing inside of that sheep would be an invisible parasite that would eventually cause death," Darryl went on. "So I have to look for specific signs of the presence of this parasite, test the sheep for the parasite, and then, if it's there, give the sheep medicine."[2]

Insert mind-blown emoji here. Instantly I thought, *That's us. We are those sheep* [Ezekiel 34:30–31; Mark 6:34], *and those dangers are pride—both visible and invisible. And hidden pride in our lives is something we need to let the Shepherd identify, test, and treat!*

TIME TO LOOK CLOSER AND GET REAL

Okay, pause with me now, and listen close.

I am with you in this. We all experience sicknesses from time to time, and it's never good to ignore them. What starts as minor misery, untreated, can turn into excruciating pain. But if we identify the sicknesses, we can learn how to deal with them and get through them—maybe conquer them—and live stronger lives.

How can we determine whether we are plagued by hidden pride? Here are some self-reflection questions to consider. I would suggest answering them yourself first, then going to trusted people in your life and getting their take. What have they observed in you? Compare the responses and see if there is consistency or tension.

1. When I am celebrated, how do I feel?
2. When I experience failure, how do I respond?
3. When I win or am right about something, what words do I say (perhaps only in my mind) about myself?
4. What words or thoughts do I have about the person who was wrong?

Hidden pride shows up in emotions of extremes within the heart—anger, jealousy, condescension, shame. The fact that pride is hidden in the heart is what makes it so dangerous. "Out of sight, out of mind," right? In this case what's out of sight is in the heart, buried deep.

Keep being brave with me here. What's actually in your heart?

When you are celebrated, do you feel an overwhelming sense that you are entitled to your success?

When you experience failure, is your internal response bitterness that you didn't get what you deserved?

When you win or are right, maybe you think, *Of course I won. I always win. Winning is what I do.*

Or, *You bet I'm right. How could anyone even think I could possibly be wrong about this? Don't they know who I am?*

When other people are wrong or lose, maybe you think, *Well, sucks to be them.*

Or, *I'm not surprised they're wrong. Now they'll learn their lesson, thinking they can catch, question, or doubt me.*

Notice the level of distortion in each of the responses—the overvaluation of yourself and the undervaluation of other people.

I am grateful to Dr. Alison Cook, a faith-based psychologist, and Jim Cress, a licensed therapist and one of my cohosts of the *Therapy & Theology* podcast, for lending their expertise to this discussion.[3] They affirmed that it is natural to feel elated (happy) or dejected (unhappy), but when those emotions are taken to extremes, they can be harmful.

"Pride is often a form of entitlement," said Dr. Cook. "It's elation without gratitude or acknowledgment of God." Jim explained that it's healthy to celebrate personal wins, but as we do, we can "choose to humble ourselves in gratitude to God for our win."

Looking at the other extreme, Dr. Cook said, "Ego-driven dejection, such as 'They'll never give me the credit I deserve' or 'I'll never be good enough' are other hidden forms of pride." Jim has observed clients who default to a victim mentality when they're rejected, and others who feel a sense of shame over their success or guilt when they are celebrated. He also explained that there are "levels of dejection" we can feel; it's not always "total dejection," which I think is helpful to remember. Hidden in these various "levels of dejection" is a seed of pride that can take root in our hearts and minds.

Hidden pride is so cunning and difficult because the conversation takes place in the chambers of the human heart, where there is no accountability. No mirror. No evidence to speak of. Interestingly, this is exactly why the ancient Hebrews were so concerned with the condition of the heart. The Hebrew word for *heart* is *lēb,* and it was understood as the source of vitality, volition, impulse, and feeling. In other words, it was both the place where feelings were felt and decisions were made.[4] So we have to be brave enough to explore our hearts, be honest about what's there, and address it. It requires immense vulnerability and courage.

> WE HAVE TO BE BRAVE ENOUGH TO EXPLORE OUR HEARTS, BE HONEST ABOUT WHAT'S THERE, AND ADDRESS IT.

As I wrote this, I honestly thought I was in a great place with hidden pride. But then something in my heart was exposed and I realized how dangerous any form of pride can be.

I had the opportunity to serve a church as they were walking through a pastoral transition. Their senior pastor had resigned, and the church needed people who could help preach through a sermon series. They invited me to preach, and it went so well that they invited me back a few more times. Then they asked that I join the small pool of applicants for their interim pastor position. I did, and, honestly, I was pretty sure I was a shoo-in. Given my academic background and the way the church responded to my preaching, it felt like a great fit.

A month later I got a call with their decision, and I could tell right away that I didn't get the job. It was definitely the "It's not you, it's me" vibe from a breakup moment. Awesome.

I processed this letdown with some close friends and moved on. I was in a great place. I wasn't upset. I didn't feel like I had an ounce of hidden pride. I had responded as graciously as I could and added the church to my prayer list because I genuinely wanted the best for them.

A month later I saw a pastor announce on social media that he'd been named the interim pastor at this church. The pastor was truly amazing—educated, winsome, theologically sound. When I saw that announcement, something happened inside me that revealed hidden pride. My heart reaction was,

What does he have that I don't?

I'm pretty sure I'm just as smart.

I'm confident that my communication skills are just as good—honestly, probably a little better.

Yeah, this makes no sense. Whatever.

I promise you, not a few minutes after I filed all this away into the chambers of my heart, a friend who knew me well and had seen the news called me. "How are you feeling?" he asked.

I paused. I had two options. Honesty or hiding.

Thankfully the Holy Spirit worked in me, and I chose honesty, exposing my hidden pride. It had been hijacking my heart, leading me to think of myself more highly than I should and less of others than I should.

My friend listened to me in silence as I got it all out—sharing my frustration, anger, and confusion. To be honest, I don't even remember what he said in response. I just remember that he listened to my pain and was a witness to my hurt and that the conversation ended how our talks usually do.

"I love you, bro," he told me. "Grateful for you."

And I replied, "Love ya too. Always here for you."

After I hung up, I was left alone in thought. And what kept going through my mind was, *Wow, this could have gone terribly wrong in my heart.* Bitterness and resentment could have settled in. Thoughts of superiority and condescension could have pervaded.

I walked out of my home study and found my wife. I gave her a big hug and said I loved her. I walked over to my toddler daughter and swooped her up in my arms and gave her a kiss. Then I walked back into my study, sat at my desk, and just said in my heart, *Thank you, Jesus.*

It was interesting what happened in my body as I processed through this. In the moment I was in turmoil, the weight that had settled in my soul slowly lifted off.

It started with that phone call with my friend.

Then it was the hug from my wife.

Next, it was my daughter's kiss.

Finally, it was the moment I just expressed gratitude to Jesus. That was when I found peace.

Hidden pride can strike anyone, anywhere. If we can be aware of how it hits us and the symptoms it causes, we have the opportunity to choose honesty instead of keeping it hidden.

This is my invitation to you to be honest with yourself, and honesty requires humility.

WE'RE BASICALLY DEALING WITH POISON HERE

Later in this book, we're going to talk about how humility is the soil we need for cultivating Christian virtues. The soil of humility in our lives is the perfect place for the fruit of the Spirit to grow, be nurtured, and mature (Galatians 5). Every good farmer pays close attention to the condition of his soil, checking to see if outside forces have somehow corrupted it, because corrupted soil bears

> **THE SOIL OF HUMILITY IN OUR LIVES IS THE PERFECT PLACE FOR THE FRUIT OF THE SPIRIT TO GROW, BE NURTURED, AND MATURE.**

spoiled fruit, or no fruit. When pride is planted in the good soil of humility, it can corrupt the soil and derail us as we grow in godliness.

Dietrich von Hildebrand, a German philosopher and theologian who resisted the Nazis, referred to pride as a "primal sin," one that "inwardly contaminates all intrinsically good dispositions and robs every virtue of its value before God."[5]

This is so important. One reason pride is so dangerous is that it has the ability to twist godly virtues into deadly, self-serving vices. On the outside it may look like we are living out the fruit of the Spirit, but on the inside, we are leveraging it to meet our own selfish ambition and vain conceit. *Love, joy, peace, patience, kindness, goodness, faithfulness, gentleness, and self-control are all great, as long as they serve a greater purpose—my self-exaltation.*

In other words, idolatry.

Pride is the road that brings us to this point. It distorts our vision, it corrupts our thoughts and desires, and it ultimately leads us to fullblown idolatry. Friend, where idolatry is present, peace is poisoned.

Okay, so we know now that pride is basically poison and it can totally sneak up on us. What's the best way to protect ourselves from such a danger?

Study it, understand it, and outplay it.

PRIDE IN SCRIPTURE: A DEEP DIVE

First off, let's define pride. It is "an unwarranted attitude of confidence" or "an unhealthy elevated view of one's self-abilities, or possessions."[6]

In the Old Testament, one of the most commonly used Hebrew words to describe pride is *gaon*, which can be translated as "height, eminence, majesty, or pride."[7] It can be used literally or metaphorically to describe pride and ambition (Proverbs 8:13, 16:18).

Did you notice *height* in that previous list? Yep, the biblical authors associate pride with height and elevation, and that connection is really important. We'll get to that in a minute.

In the New Testament, there are a number of related words used to convey the pride of humanity. Take Mark 7:21–23, for instance: "From within, out of people's hearts, come evil thoughts, sexual immoralities, thefts, murders, adulteries, greed, evil actions, deceit, self-indulgence, envy, slander, *pride* [*hyperēphania*], and foolishness. All these evil things come from within and defile a person."

Check out 2 Corinthians 10:4–5: "The weapons of our warfare are not of the flesh, but are powerful through God for the demolition of strongholds. We demolish arguments and every *proud* [*hypsōma*] thing that is raised up against the knowledge of God, and we take every thought captive to obey Christ."

Pride comes from within and corrupts the heart, which in turn defiles the person, and pride attempts to raise us above the wisdom of God. Interestingly, the Greek word translated as "proud" in 2 Corinthians 10:5 (*hypsōma*) is often related to the "heavenly realm of God" elsewhere in Scripture (Psalm 68:19, 102:20; Isaiah 40:26; from the Greek translation of the Hebrew Old Testament).[8]

That same word appears in Isaiah 2:17 (again, Greek translation), which sheds more light on pride's connection with humility and idolatry: "The haughtiness of man shall be humbled, and the lofty pride of men shall be brought low, and the LORD alone will be exalted in that day" (ESV).[9]

Okay, I know we're in the thick of some in-depth Bible exploration. Stick with me here so we can make a few connections.

The fact that pride is related to elevation and height is important because the same concept is true of the heavenly dwelling place
of God. This means pride takes us on a journey of trying to elevate
ourselves to be like God, to reach the same heights at which he
dwells! It's a place we can't force ourselves into; it's available to us
through invite only. And the invite has a prerequisite: humility.

Forcing ourselves into this place is like soaring up into air too
thin for us to breathe in without an oxygen tank, like catapulting
ourselves into outer space with no gear. It is the Creator's domain,
and we, the created, are simply not meant to be there through our
own means. We can go there only if God elevates us and equips us.

This is a principle we see throughout Scripture. In Genesis 11
people gathered together and, in pride, tried to build a ziggurat
tower to ascend into the heavens. They attempted to force God to
come down as they went up. God wouldn't stand for it. He essentially "grounded" them by diversifying their tongues and spreading
them out across the world.

We see this same pride-height connection reflected in idol
worship. Amos 5:26 says, "You have *lifted up* the shrine of your
king, the pedestal of your idols . . . which you have made for yourselves" (NIV). In this verse the idols are being physically lifted up.
This serves as a visual example of how the exaltation of an idol, or
ourselves, is the act of assigning honor and authority to someone
other than God. We are lifting these things up high above and
over God.

Another idolatry callout moment in Daniel 5 lays it out even
more clearly for us: "You . . . have not humbled your heart, . . . but
you have *lifted up yourself* against the Lord of heaven. . . . You have
praised the gods of silver and gold . . . which do not see or hear or
know, but the God in whose hand is your breath, . . . you have not
honored" (vv. 22–23 ESV).

While we're not dealing with actual idols on pedestals today, many of us are dealing with self-absorption. In our hearts we are "lifting up ourselves," making ourselves the focal point, the authority, and the ultimate source for meeting our own needs.

Okay, let's pause for a recap, shall we?

Pride lifts us high and invites us onto the cliff. It promises safety, security, and stability, but all along its intent is to push us off the cliff toward our self-destruction. This can happen when we lack self-awareness.

Humility, on the other hand, is a guardrail of safety; it is something that truly protects us. It grounds us and enables us to enjoy the beauty of the mountaintop view with the self-awareness we need to stay safe and secure.

When we turn back to the origin story of humanity, we find that God created man by forming him from "the dust" of the ground and breathing life into him (Genesis 2:7). Notice where humanity was created from—the "dust" and the "ground." Interestingly, the word *humility* comes from the Latin word *humus*, which means the ground or soil.[10]

Theologian and author Richard Foster summarized the take-away here like this: "With humility we are brought back to earth. We don't think of ourselves higher than we should."[11] Part of being "brought back to earth" is self-awareness of who we are and who we are not.

The beauty of humility is that it is where God breathes life into us. When we are in this posture, he swoops down from the heights of heaven to pick us up and elevate us with him as children of the King, placing us where we can experience true peace.

But pride robs us of the possibility of this peace.

Pride tells us we can do what we want ourselves.

When pride creeps into our lives, it distorts our perception of

God. We find ourselves disoriented because we've lost sight of him. We are unable to view ourselves or other people the right way.

Pride invites us to lie to ourselves and feel good about it.

If you want power, you need to make money moves. The more money you have, the more power you can wield.

If you want strength, you need to minimize everyone around you. If you show their weakness, you can exalt yourself and your strength.

The promise of pride is never true, and it is never worth the pain it brings.

Here is the key aspect of pride we need to remember: *pride takes us outside of truth.* It distorts what is true and real by placing us at the center of the world. It pushes us toward the thought, *What's best for me is what's best for everyone else.* It swaps out *The Bible tells me so* for *My heart tells me so.*

Pride blinds us, then tells us we can see perfectly. We get convinced that we're fine, we can trust our instincts—never minding that they're pride-hijacked instincts. Pride makes us its unwitting followers, then leads us to self-exaltation.

The scary thing is, as high as pride leads us is as far as we'll fall once it pushes us off the cliff to perish. This is the path of pride.

I'm going to tell you about another uncomfortable moment of hidden pride from my life. I can't say that it's easy for me to share—but humility and honesty go hand in hand, so here we go.

In 2021, after the COVID pandemic lockdown, our three boys were returning to in-person school after a long stretch of at-home school. This was a relief for Britt and me but a full-on tragedy for our one-and-a-half-year-old daughter, EmJ. She had gotten used to her "bubbies" (what she calls her older brothers) being home all day every day, entertaining her and playing with her.

That first day the boys went to school, poor little EmJ was

distraught and depressed. When it was time for them to come back on the bus, Britt walked outside with EmJ to wait for them. What happened next was honestly magical.

As soon as the bus pulled up, EmJ started waddling toward it, hurrying more with each step. When she saw them come off the bus, she began running as fast as her little legs would let her, screaming, "Bubbies! I'm here! BUBBIES!!"

All three boys saw her running toward them and started screaming, "Emmy! I see you! EMMY!!!" They ran toward her, too, and when they met, they embraced, and all was good in the world again.

Britt caught the whole thing on video and it was truly special. So special that she shared it that night on her Instagram account (@almostindianwife, where she typically posts content about the complexity of blending cultures in relationships).

The next morning Britt's phone wouldn't turn on, which was weird. My phone had missed calls, texts, and notifications. As I read through them, I saw things like

JOEL! Your kids!
Beyoncé's mom posted!
Jay Shetty Posted!
Viola Davis posted!
JOELLLLLLLLL, JANET JACKSON POSTED.

It went on and on. The video had gone viral. So viral that the notifications actually broke Britt's phone and it had to be restarted.

The next forty-eight hours were wild, with celebrities and news channels continually posting about the video. By the end of the week, it had over ten million views (today, it's around twenty-five million views). People kept commenting that seeing genuine love between siblings reminded them of what they once had, what they wish they had, or what they were willing to fight for to get back. It was extraordinary.

Before long, Britt looked at me one evening and said, "Joey . . . Kelly Clarkson!"

I was like, "Yeah, I love Kelly Clarkson. Big fan."

She said, "No . . . *The Kelly Clarkson Show* wants to interview our family!"

We were all ecstatic.

In the lead-up to the interview, Britt had a pre-call with the production team.

"Our family is ready!" she told them. "My husband and I are so excited to be on the show with Kelly and our kiddos!"

"Oh . . . your husband? Was he in the video?" someone from the team asked.

Confused, Britt said, "Well, no. He was working at the time."

The team gently suggested that it'd perhaps be best not to have "the husband" in the interview so the focus would stay on the kids, the ones who'd made the moment beautiful. They thought Britt should be present, too, because she had taken the video.

Britt looked over at me, checking in.

Without thinking, I said, "Of course! That totally makes sense. You guys go on the show and crush it. I can run our technology and keep the dogs out of the way."

And that's what happened.

As I hid behind a wall in our kitchen, my wife and kids talked to Kelly Clarkson about the bus reunion moment and the sweet closeness they shared. They were awesome. I was thrilled for them, amazed by them, and so proud of the way they brought joy to the world.

The next day, it hit me. *This is my family. These are my kids. And yet I was uninvited from that special moment.*

Hidden pride. It shows up in some of the most unseen and unexpected places.

The day before, I'd had peace, but now there was turmoil in my soul, robbing me of that peace. While I loved the spotlight on my wife and kids, I also was wondering, *But what about me?*

Now, the question itself isn't bad; it's super honest. I want you to know it is not only okay but also *vital* that we are honest with ourselves and our loved ones.

But the Enemy of our souls wants to take that honest question and keep it hidden in our hearts so resentment can take root and bitterness can develop.

So, what did I do?

I talked to my wife about it. I called a couple of trusted friends and confessed that my heart was sad and my ego had taken a shot.

Then I turned my focus away from those feelings. I sat down and watched the video of my wife and kids doing that interview and allowed it to fill my heart with joy. I let it remind me of the immeasurable good my children had brought into the world and how proud I was of them.

You see, the Enemy's desire was for me to keep all that negative emotion internalized and bottled up so it would consume my heart and eventually disrupt the peace in my household. This is the kind of thing the Enemy desires, and he loves using pride as a tool for his schemes.

Have you ever wondered why the Enemy works in this way? I think there's a reason for this. He went down the path of pride himself.

And, in fact, if we look closely at his story, we will better understand how "pride traps" work and how we can avoid them.

Let's grasp who this Enemy of our souls is so we can protect our souls from him.

CHAPTER 7

"I DON'T TRUST LIMITS": PRIDE CONTINUED

I'M NOT A cat person. I've never been a cat person, and I'll never be a cat person. It doesn't help that I am extremely allergic to cats—but even if I weren't, I know in my heart I'd still be a dog person.

When I first came to work at Proverbs 31 Ministries, one of the first questions the team asked me was if I was a cat person. I was in shock. I expected questions about theology, ministry, heck, even sports—not my allegiance to cats.

My answer was simple and quick: "You know what they say— 'Curiosity killed the cat.' So I prefer avoiding cats, their curiosity, and all the turmoil that comes with them. I am a dog person."

Do they keep a spreadsheet tracking each staff member's status on this issue? Maybe. (And if they did, I'd be happy to report that I turned the tide toward #teamdog, and, at the time of this writing, we are still firmly in the lead.)

Curiosity is an interesting thing. Curiosity in and of itself isn't bad. But most of us know someone who let their curiosity get the better of them. If you don't know anyone like that, just head over to our friend Google and type in "curious cat videos." Enjoy.

As I was writing this, I got curious myself about why cats have this behavior trait, and I learned something interesting: cats' curiosity is connected to their survival. It keeps their "senses sharp for hunting, finding mates, seeking out shelter, staying warm, and caring for the young."[1] So curiosity is good for them—but only to an extent. Things go badly for these feline friends (not *my* friends, of course) when they try to do things *beyond* their limits.

The same goes for us. We often buck against the idea of limits, but the reality is, curiosity without limits will eventually lead to some sort of loss.

CURIOSITY TO THE EXTREME

I think this is why God gave Adam and Eve boundaries in the garden of Eden. He basically told them, "You can go ahead and eat of every tree. They're all good, and you should enjoy the pleasures of my good creation. But one catch: there's this one tree that is off limits. Don't eat that fruit. Everything else is yours to enjoy; just this one thing is a no."

God seemed to understand their human curiosity. But he also knew that curiosity without boundaries could get them into trouble, so he established boundaries for them. Oh, and if they got confused, no worries. God would be with them in Eden, so they could always just go ask him.

I would go so far as to say God encouraged Adam and Eve's curiosity and gave them tangible ways to express it. "All the animals in Eden, go ahead and check them out! While you're at it, name them too."

So when the serpent (whom we will come to know as Satan throughout Scripture) came to Eve, he attacked the good, God-given curiosity of humanity. God, in his wisdom, had given them what they needed to handle this deception—firm boundaries. But curiosity got the best of our first parents. Let's follow the progression of the conversation and see how curiosity led to pride, and how pride led to idolatry.

"The serpent was the most cunning of all the wild animals that the LORD God had made. He said to the woman, 'Did God really say, "You can't eat from any tree in the garden"?'" (Genesis 3:1).

"Did God really say . . . ?" is a question posed out of curious doubt. So the serpent, "the most cunning of all the wild animals," positioned himself not as a villain but as an innocent bystander asking a curious question.

The seemingly innocent curiosity of the serpent invited Eve into being curious about the validity of God's truth. Eve was hooked, wheels turning. The astute serpent prodded further and denied the consequence of disobedience, then suggested that God was actually holding something good back from Eve and Adam.

"No! You will certainly not die," the serpent said to the woman. "In fact, God knows that when you eat it your eyes will be opened and you will be like God, knowing good and evil." The woman saw that the tree was good for food and delightful to look at, and that it was desirable for obtaining wisdom. So she took some of its fruit and ate it; she also gave some to her husband, who was with her, and he ate it. (Genesis 3:4–6)

When the genuine curiosity of Eve and Adam hit the boundaries God had established, they had a choice: trust in the goodness and truth of God, or explore beyond God's boundary lines in case God was not being truthful.

Is God holding something back from us? What if he doesn't want us to have true enjoyment? Is God being overprotective and unfair?

These are all curious questions that can lead to serious consequences.

Now, hear me on this: the problem isn't having the questions. The problem is what we sometimes do with them.

Eve and Adam let these types of thoughts and questions move them from genuine curiosity into pride. They began thinking they deserved to "be like God," and this prideful belief guided their hands to the fruit and nudged them to that disastrous first bite. As they ate of the fruit, they fell into full-blown idolatry, attempting to replace God's authority with their own.

It didn't have to go this way.

Remember, all Adam and Eve had to do was allow their God-given curiosity to turn them back to God so they could ask him for wisdom. Instead, they let it lead them to sin against him. But twisting something good (in this case, curiosity) into something that leads to sin is how the Evil One works. He inverts and corrupts the goodness of God's creation. He often does this by turning our hearts and ambitions inward, toward ourselves, when our hearts and ambitions ought to be aimed outward, toward God.

We really shouldn't be surprised that the serpent used curiosity as his weapon of choice against God's children, because it serves as the perfect entryway to pride. Curiosity was in fact the very thing that turned the serpent from a loyal servant of God into an idolater and Enemy.

THE DARKEST OF ORIGIN STORIES

Do you know much about Satan's origin story? Few of us do. It's not exactly a top choice for Sunday school, right? Plus, it's told in pieces throughout several places in the Bible, so it can be confusing. Well, we're going to bring all those pieces together here, see where things went so terribly wrong, and learn all we can from it.

Sneak preview for you: curiosity, pride, and idolatry were all deeply interconnected with the sin of the ancient serpent.

Now, you may be thinking, *Why are we talking about this? Aren't we figuring out humility here?*

It may sound surprising, but looking at this will help us understand more about why humility can feel so far away and why the idea of dependence on God can freak us out.

Our preoccupation with self runs deep, y'all. It is so familiar that we don't even see it. And we can wind up in mental patterns that carry us away from God and from seeing him and everything else rightly—away from humility and all its benefits. So we're going to build up more awareness of what can happen, using an extreme (scary negative) example, so we can better identify red flags in our own lives.

Okay, first of all, let's talk about Satan's names. Scripture refers to him in a variety of ways:

- the serpent (Genesis)
- the prince of demons (Matthew 9:34, 12:24; Mark 3:22; Luke 11:15 ESV)
- the prince of the power of the air (Ephesians 2:2 ESV)
- the god of this age (2 Corinthians 4:4)

Genesis refers to him simply as a "serpent," but the Hebrew word used there, *nakhash*, indicates he is actually a supernatural being. There's a lot going on with this Hebrew word—it can mean serpent; divine throne guardian; or having a shining, bronze, or fiery appearance. And here in Genesis, all three of these meanings are at play.[2]

In the Ancient Near Eastern world, the *nakhash* was a symbol for a "divine throne Guardian."[3] And Genesis 3 puts this "guardian" in Eden, which can be considered the temple home of Yahweh, the first image of the Holy Place where God's throne resides. This means the serpent was near God's throne and responsible to guard it.

We can see how the shining fiery element fits, too, when we look at a divine throne room scene in Isaiah 6. It describes angelic beings guarding the throne of God, using the Hebrew word *saraph*, which can refer to a kind of serpent or a fiery serpent shape (Numbers 21:8).

So, the overall take here: at the beginning of Satan's narrative, he was a supernatural being, a guardian cherub who spent his days gazing on the throne of God.

There are two more places in Scripture that unpack the origin story of Satan: Ezekiel 28 and Isaiah 14. In both places he is described as a shining or bright star, which ties back to the serpent of Genesis 3 and the "shining, bronze, or fiery appearance" meaning of the Hebrew word (*nakhash*) used for him there. Ezekiel 28 and Isaiah 14 each offer a prophecy about a human king, but inside those prophecies is another layer that tells the background story of Satan's downfall—specifically how his curiosity created pride in his heart, which led to idolatry and an act of rebellion against God.

We can relate to the curiosity part, can't we? Sometimes curiosity sparks in us when we see something we want but can't have. In the parking lot of my local gym, I've noticed a red Porsche and daydreamed about what it would be like to drive it. I could see myself opening up the door, getting in, feeling the engine turn over, and then hitting that gas pedal as I peel out of the parking lot to a crowd of eyes watching in amazement.

Maybe, instead of a Porsche, you daydream about an Instagram-perfect house. The design is on point, with every room laid out with Joanna Gaines–like style and expertise. The spacious master suite feels like your own luxurious apartment. The huge backyard has a view to die for and an inviting porch swing, where you can sit and watch your family play and laugh and live their best lives.

Now, there is a difference between the curiosity of imagining what it would be like and deciding you actually deserve that thing and will do whatever it takes to get it.

What if I decided to break into the Porsche and steal it?

What if you decided to show up at that house and demand the family that lives there move out because your crew was moving in?

Absurd!

But curiosity without limits is absurd. Pride distorts our vision and compromises our conscience. Pride takes what is absurd and suggests it is what we deserve.

> PRIDE DISTORTS OUR VISION AND COMPROMISES OUR CONSCIENCE.

At some point, the serpent guarding God's throne allowed his curiosity about that throne to lead him into pride and the belief that he deserved to sit on it and become the king of the kingdom. This is idolatry.

Here's how it played out, according to Ezekiel 28:12–17.[4]

Satan was a being of immense beauty. God covered him in precious gems, which signified special priority and privilege, and made him an "*anointed* guardian cherub" (v. 14). God called him "blameless" (v. 15).

Then things took a tragic turn.

At some point, after gazing at God's throne day after day, Satan's curiosity about it turned his heart to pride. God reported it like this: "Your heart became proud because of your beauty; for the sake of your splendor you corrupted your wisdom" (v. 17).

Satan's splendor and beauty caused him to think of himself *a lot*—like, obsessively. Pride creates an overly elevated view of ourselves. It robs us of our self-awareness and tempts us to magnify ourselves and minimize everyone else. We've talked before about how pride distorts our vision and corrupts the good soil of humility. This is exactly what happened to Satan.

According to Isaiah 14:13–14, Satan thought, "I will ascend to the heavens; I will set up my throne above the stars of God. I will sit on the mount of the gods' assembly, in the remotest parts of the North. I will ascend above the highest clouds; *I will make myself like the Most High.*"[5]

The pride of Satan led him to act in idolatry against God.

When the early church father Origen commented on this, he connected Satan's "arrogance and pride of heart" with his corruption and ultimate downfall. Origen said Satan seemed to think that "the privileges which he enjoyed when he lived blamelessly were his own and not given to him by God."[6]

At the end of the day, Satan fell into self-deception and came to believe he had the right to be God.

This is picture-perfect narcissism, which is a word that stems from the ancient Greek myth about Narcissus, who saw a reflection of his own image and fell in love with himself.[7] His obsession with himself ultimately ended in his death. The myth of Narcissus is a retelling of the story of Satan, who became obsessed with himself.[8]

We see warnings about self-deception elsewhere in Scripture, like in Galatians 6:3: "If anyone thinks they are something when they are not, they deceive themselves" (NIV).

Jim Cress once remarked that psychological research has proven that "all narcissists are self-deceived."[9] He has also clarified that there is a difference between being diagnosed with narcissistic personality disorder and having some generally narcissistic tendencies—which all of us have. One of those tendencies is self-deception. This is why we want to really consider this. If we're super caught up in ourselves, somewhere along the way we must have started fooling ourselves and buying into our own delusions.

Now, keep in mind that self-deception typically doesn't happen in an instant. The Greek word *narkaō*, which is related to our English word *narcissist*, means "to grow numb by applying pressure."[10] Over time, as we indulge in pride, create space for conceit, and allow deception in our lives, we will grow numb. And numbness is the perfect state for idolatry to take root.

Okay, let's summarize what we've seen.

Idolatry was the sin of Satan and the temptation he proposed to Adam and Eve.

The pathway to idolatry is pride. The longing of pride is ultimately to be like God.

The entrance to pride is curiosity.

BRING IT HOME

We went deep, y'all. And I promise you it will pay off. Before we close this chapter, we're going to process how all this deep Bible study applies to our lives. We aren't guardian cherubs, and we aren't walking around thinking up plots to hijack God's throne. But pride is still evident in our lives, distorting our view of ourselves and others.

So we're going to translate the trajectory of Satan to our own life situation. That might sound weird, but stay with me. And remember, we're reaching for more awareness, which can bridge us to humility and all its life-changing gifts.

CURIOSITY

We've said before that curiosity in and of itself is not bad; the problem is when curiosity has no limits. We're going to see if we're dealing with that problem by assessing the condition of our hearts.

When you see someone else receive good things—financial or material gain, a flourishing relationship, a dream come true—what is your initial unfiltered heart reaction?

Not fair!
Good for them.
Why not me?
Well, that sucks.
Of course, they would . . .

If any of these questions (or fears) come true, it can shatter any peace we hope for. Friend, I have good news for you: I see no sin here. Having these types of feelings, processing these emotions, is not wrong in God's eyes. I return often to something Lysa says: "Feelings are indicators, not dictators."[11] The best way we can respond to feelings like these is to be honest about them and address them with God (and others), allowing his light and love to interact with them.

We also should consider what our feelings *indicate*. They might be tied to a curiosity or fear, which could take the form of questions.

What if I don't have enough money?
What if I don't get the material things I'm hoping for?
What if I stay stuck in my mundane, average life forever?
What if someone I care about leaves?
What if someone important to me doesn't notice me?
What if I'm not worthy of that relationship, or I mess it up?

When we see others get what we want, it hurts, and we can't help but wonder if good things are for everyone else, not us. Deeper in our hearts, we may be asking even bigger questions, perhaps without putting them to words. Questions that mirror the scene in Eden.

Does God really have good things in store for me?
Is he holding something back? Is he being unfair?
Do I need to grab for things I want on my own? Or will he, in
    time, prove to be generous?

Again, none of this is sin. These curious questions aren't a problem, but they can lead us into a problem. Remember, Eve and Adam's questions caused them to choose between trusting in the goodness and truth of God and pridefully exploring beyond God's boundaries (the words he spoke to them) in case he was not being truthful. If we don't have humility as a limit, our curiosity can move us into pride.

PRIDE

Part of this is review, but let's make sure we've got it. Pride moves us from curiosity into an overly elevated view of ourselves and what we want. Things we desire are not just what we want or are willing to work for; they are things we feel we deserve because we think more of ourselves than we should. Pride distorts and disorients us, hijacking our ability to see clearly. Jesus referred to this kind of debilitating pride in Matthew 7 when he addressed the judgment of others, saying,

> "Why do you look at the splinter in your brother's eye but don't notice the beam of wood in your own eye? Or how can you say to your brother, 'Let me take the splinter out of your eye,' and look, there's a beam of wood in your own eye? Hypocrite! First take the beam of wood out of your eye, and then you will see clearly to take the splinter out of your brother's eye." (vv. 3–5)

I love how Bernard of Clairvaux, a son of nobility in the 1100s who chose to become a monk, talked about this passage:

The heavy, thick beam in the eye is pride of heart. It is big but not strong, swollen, not solid. It blinds the eye of the mind and blots out the truth. While it is there you cannot see yourself as you really are, or even the ideal of what you could be, but what you would like to be.[12]

Pride is a guide that promises to take you to paradise and deceitfully leads you into a prison. It prevents you from seeing yourself as you really are in light of who God is. Pride is truly a seductive sin that leads us into full-blown rebellion.

IDOLATRY

Idolatry throughout the Old Testament referred to the worship of graven images or figures, and God explicitly condemned it (Exodus 20:4–6; Deuteronomy 5:6–10).

Pride causes us to elevate ourselves over and against God; the object of our worship becomes ourselves. Pride tells us we deserve everything our eyes gaze upon and everything our hearts long for. We place our own "image"—and desires—as the ultimate priority and, in doing so, we step into full-blown idolatry.

What can we learn from all this?

Pride is a seductive sin. Humility is God's grace to overcome it.

One of the greatest weapons we have to combat pride is prayer. I have to say, I learned the power of prayer from my mom, who is the ultimate prayer warrior and my hero for so many reasons. When I was a kid and our family was going through some really hard things, I'd sometimes walk into her room and find her on her knees in prayer. She would invite me to join her and teach me to pray. And just like my mom invited me to join her in prayer, I want to invite you to join me.

> PRIDE IS A SEDUCTIVE SIN. HUMILITY IS GOD'S GRACE TO OVERCOME IT.

Here is a prayer that may be a helpful starting point as we do the deep work of weeding out pride with the help of the Holy Spirit.

Lord, my desires at times can be so strong. It's easy for me to feel consumed with longing, convinced I must have what I want when I want it. I'm obsessed with a different reality I can see myself in the middle of, one I feel I desperately need and sincerely want.

But, God, I see you as higher than all of this. Today, I choose to put you above my own desires. I give my longings to you. I'm asking you to shape and form my longings to reflect yours. And I trust in the goodness you want to bring me, in your way, that is better than anything I could dream up.

You are the God of the universe, God of my heart, and God of my future.

You are God, and I am not. And that is a very, very good thing. Amen.

The height to which pride leads us is the height from which we'll come crashing down. This was the consequence for Satan. He wanted to be the "most high," but instead he became the "most low," receiving the humiliation of crawling around the earth on his belly.[13]

> HUMILITY REFOCUSES AND ORIENTS OUR EYES CLEARLY ON GOD.

Pride distorts our vision of God. Humility refocuses and orients our eyes clearly on God.

Pride tempts us to believe that we are the pinnacle of creation. Humility reminds us that we are beautiful, loved, and cherished by God—but we are indeed the creation while he is the Creator.

Whoever exalts himself (acting on pride) will be humbled, but whoever humbles himself will be exalted (Matthew 23:12; Luke 14:11, 18:14). God's good design and directive for us is abundantly clear: "Humble yourselves before the Lord, and he will exalt you" (James 4:10).[14]

Humility is the only effective protection against and response to pride and self-deception. It makes us aware of the deceit in our hearts and teaches us how to be self-aware. It allows us to enjoy the goodness of curiosity without stepping out of God's wise limits.

> HUMILITY IS THE ONLY EFFECTIVE PROTECTION AGAINST AND RESPONSE TO PRIDE AND SELF-DECEPTION.

Remember how we started this chapter with saying, "Curiosity killed the cat"? Well, what if curiosity didn't have to kill the cat? What if curiosity doesn't have to lead us into pride and idolatry? It actually doesn't—but humility is required for that to happen. Humility gives us the limits we need to be curious without moving into destructive territory.

We'll soon dive into how we can bring it into our lives. But first, we need to disarm some lies and hesitations about humility—ones that have likely caused us to keep it at arm's length for too long.

PART 3

TRANSFORMING "MY WAY"
INTO "THE WAY OF HUMILITY"

CHAPTER 8

GRASP IT (FORGET THE LIES)

ONE OF MY favorite times of the year is the lead-up to football season. I'm an avid fantasy football player, and I take playing the game to another stratosphere. I watch practice film, have a detailed note-taking system on players, and create a drafting strategy filled with all kinds of what-if situations. I mentioned I was competitive, right?

One year, a player I had targeted to draft for my wide receiver slot was a young second-year player named Henry Ruggs. Of all my what-if situations that included injuries or trades to other teams, the one I didn't have planned was Ruggs driving under the influence and crashing his car into another vehicle, tragically killing a twenty-three-year-old woman. The same day, the team Ruggs played for released him from his NFL contract, and his entire life changed in a split second.[1]

Ruggs had it all—money, success, exciting opportunities. Then, because of a single irresponsible decision, multiple lives tragically changed forever.

There are countless people in the public eye who've had de-stabilizing experiences that have affected their daily lives.

At the live-recorded 2022 Oscars, actor Will Smith shocked the world with a sudden act of rage and violence. When Chris Rock made a joke about Smith's wife, Smith immediately rushed onstage and slapped him. He later tied his behavior to childhood trauma and ongoing anger problems.[2]

In the spring of 2022, the iconic actor Bruce Willis announced to the world his diagnosis of aphasia—a neurological disorder that impacts the ability to speak, write, and communicate in general. Sadly, the Willis family later announced his health was in further decline and he had received another diagnosis, frontotemporal dementia.[3] Bruce and his loved ones are experiencing destabilization due to these unexpected and certainly unwanted medical diagnoses.

Actress Zendaya has publicly opened up about her struggle with anxiety. In a 2020 Instagram post, she shared, "Just had the worst panic attack I've ever had in my life. I am broken right now."[4] In interviews, she has further explained, "[It's] something I deal with; I have anxiety. I already know after this interview is over, I'm going to spiral about it for weeks. . . . I definitely don't have it under control yet."[5]

Despite having achieved monumental success, these people have still experienced a loss of control, stability, and security in multiple ways—emotionally, physically, relationally.

The same is true for the everyday people in our lives.

And the same is true for you and me.

I know it's daunting to face all of this. I feel it too. How can we accept that we can't keep everything together, and that weakness is inevitable? That no amount of power will ease the constant ache of insecurity in our souls, and that pride seems to be a natural response woven into our DNA?

All of this is straight-up *hard*.

Then add to it your innate hesitation and flat-out skepticism to jump toward humility as a solution. *Come on. Isn't humility for losers?* Be honest. It's been lurking in the back of your mind. It for sure has been in mine!

There are legitimate reasons for us to feel hesitant right now, and it's important that we don't ignore them.

THE WALL OF HESITATION

Let's just lay them out here, shall we? You may have thought:

- *Humility is for losers.*
- *Humility is for the weak and powerless.*
- *Humility is a fast track to humiliation.*
- *Humility is great for them but not for me.*
- *Humility is an unfair ask, and the fact you are asking it of me makes you an unfair person.*

I've thought and struggled with these issues continually, so much that I didn't want to write this message because I feared everyone would stop reading and close the book. (It took me a while to feel confident enough even to share the early stages of this message with close friends!) I've followed through with it because every time I come back to Scripture, I'm convinced this is the lost, hidden way to the experiences we're all longing for.

And I've got to say, the negative thoughts above reflect the lies we've been told about humility. They've come from a world that doesn't understand it.

Most of that list boils down to having a low, less-than view of yourself. But humility isn't self-loathing; it has nothing to do with devaluing who you are. If it ever leads you to low self-esteem, consider that a red flag that what you have is not biblical humility.

> LIVING A LIFE OF HUMILITY DOESN'T MEAN YOU HAVE TO LAY DOWN CONFIDENCE OR COURAGE. IT ACTUALLY GIVES YOU *MORE* OF THESE THINGS.

Living a life of humility also doesn't mean you have to lay down confidence or courage. It actually gives you *more* of these things. We will be exploring this amazing reality in later chapters.

Am I saying that if you learn and live out biblical humility, you will be miraculously protected from pain? No. Unfortunately, that's not how life works. People can still weaponize it, like so many other things. I have experienced heartache associated with humility when prideful people chose to use it against me. But even here, the problem wasn't humility; it was the people who weaponized humility for their own selfish gain and vain conceit.

So, if humility doesn't bring about self-loathing or rob you of confidence and courage, what does it do?

We've touched on this before, back in chapter 1.

Instead of leaving us unstable and weak, humility makes us steadier and stronger. Instead of squashing down our strengths and potential, it helps the best of who we are flourish. It helps us have healthy, fulfilling relationships. And it gives us confidence to face our fears and courage to walk through our hurts.

Okay. So *that* we can go for.

How do we get there, exactly? What would it look like to move in that direction?

MOVING INTO THE HUMILITY MINDSET

There are three basic steps to moving into a humility mindset and lifestyle:

1. Becoming aware of our need for humility.
2. Accepting our need for humility and then doing something about it.
3. Applying all of this to our lives by joining Jesus on a daily journey of humility.

AWARENESS

First, we need to be shaken out of our current *self-made* perspective with a reality check. We've got to wake up our brains to what's really going on in the universe—and what our place is in it.

This is like when I go to the beach (even though, let it be known, I am more of a mountain person than a beach person), and I am captured by the beauty and vastness of the scene. I can't escape the reality before me. The force and rhythm of the waves. The receding sun painting the sky with vibrant colors. The countless forms of life teeming beneath the surface. The world around me becoming darker and colder with the rays of light slowly fading behind the rippling waters. I become aware of how finite I am and how dependent I am on God as I catch a glimpse of how he reigns over his world.

Awareness is a beautiful thing because it brings about proper orientation. We stand in wonder at the infinite and great God who, in a breath, brought about all creation. The kindness of a God who chose to breathe life into humans. The never-ending love of a God who sent his own Son to pay a price we owed, dying a death we deserved, all so we could receive his righteousness and join his family.

Humility is fundamentally an intimate awareness of the magnitude of our

> HUMILITY IS FUNDAMENTALLY AN INTIMATE AWARENESS OF THE MAGNITUDE OF OUR SIN AND THE MAGNIFICENCE OF GOD'S GRACE.

sin and the magnificence of God's grace. If we are not first captivated by an awareness of who God truly is and who we are in light
of him, the humble life is impossible.

ACCEPTANCE

It's one thing to be aware of something as true and quite
another to personally accept it, saying "This thing is true *for me*,
and I will now change course because of it."

This is like when my nine-year-old son, Levi (you may remember him as the Leviathan), first got glasses and figured out how to
randomly "lose" the glasses all over the house. He was aware that he
needed them, but he refused to accept that he was going to have to
wear them. It wasn't until he faced the consequences of not wearing
them (headaches, inability to see movies, trouble reading) that he
changed his ways. He had to move from awareness to acceptance.

When it comes to humility, I think the first step of awareness
is somewhat easy. We can logically lay out all the reasons, in light
of God's greatness, we ought to be humble. That is what we've been
doing up until this point in the book.

The next step of accepting, "Yes, humility is something I personally need," tends to be more difficult. Just like Levi "forgetting"
his glasses all over the house, I tend to forget humility all over the
place in my life. I struggle with accepting that it's something I
actually need.

Sometimes I'll start thinking that humility will become an
invitation for others to hurt me—and why should I accept something that could bring more hurt into my life? Well, hold on. While
humility may make it possible to get hurt, the same is true if we
don't have humility. As we've discussed, no matter how much control, strength, and power we have, hurt will always still be around
the corner.

What I need to pursue isn't something to prevent hurt in my

life. I need to pursue something that will *help me get through the hurt.*

When we accept our need for humility, we are making room for the very thing that will gently and kindly walk with us as we navigate through the hurts of our lives caused by fear, instability, lack of control, and weakness.

And so we resolve to start moving our thoughts and actions that direction.

APPLICATION

Here we are at the pivot point—living it out. Really and truly doing it. We're going to do a theological deep dive into humility. But learning a theology that can't be lived is a tragedy.

To begin with, instead of asking "How do I achieve humility?" we need to ask, "How do I live a life of humility?"

The first question places humility in the category of something that can be achieved, accomplished, or won so we can then move on from it. This is extremely dangerous. At the root of this mindset is pride. We can't simply make humility a tool we wield to carry out our purposes and achieve our ambitions.

The second question expresses an aim to be on the journey of humility, acknowledging that we cannot win or achieve it. In fact, developing it is completely impossible for us to do on our own! The good news is that we don't have to.

Augustine of Hippo wrote, "Humility comes from elsewhere, from the One who, being the Most High, wished to empty Himself for us."[6]

Humility comes from Jesus. Living with humility is made possible only when we live in and through the life of the one who was humble in all his ways. He's the only one who can truly live a life of humility.

And yet we as humans are meant for this kind of existence! As we've mentioned before, humans were first created in the context of humility.

The Hebrew word for man/humanity is *adam* and is related to the Hebrew word *adamah*, which refers to the ground or soil.[7] The same concept shows up in Latin. The English words *human* and *humility* have a common Latin connection with *humus*; we've said before that *humus* refers to the ground or soil. So, in both the Hebrew and Latin languages, these words connect the concepts of humanity, humility, and being grounded.

Paul warned his fellow believers, "Let anyone who thinks that he stands take heed lest he fall" (1 Corinthians 10:12 ESV). If our pride leads us into a falsely elevated view of ourselves, we remove ourselves from the soil and the ground that brings us stability.

G. K. Chesterton said something similar when he warned of a type of self-enjoyment that extends our ego to the infinite. Chesterton said the opposite should be true for us as Christians as we discover that "the fullest possible enjoyment is to be found by reducing our ego to zero."[8]

The words of both the apostle Paul and Chesterton tell us that the safest place for the believer to be is deeply planted in the rich soil of humility, which is in fact the very origin and home of humanity.

Scholar and pastor Eugene Peterson described it for us well: "Humility means staying close to the ground (*humus*), to people, to everyday life, to what is happening with all its down-to-earthness."[9]

THE POWER OF A PERSPECTIVE SHIFT

I have a friend who, from a young age, had a heart for serving others and felt called to become a doctor. Always the smartest student in his class, he got into a great university and completed a premed program. He faced difficulties along the way, but God opened the door for him to get into medical school, and he progressed to the stage of taking the board exam. Passing this Goliath, as he called it, was the key to getting into a good medical residency program and finally achieving his yearslong goal of becoming a doctor.

He took the test, and the results were less then desirable.

So he studied more and took the test again. The results were *still* below what he needed to pass.

This was soul crushing for my friend. To make things worse, he watched his friends pass their exams and get accepted to their residency programs. Seeing them celebrate their achievements just rubbed salt in the wound.

He eventually recognized that he'd done all he could to reach his goal and that, while his desire to be a doctor was a good thing, God had something better in store for him.

He became *aware* of this reality.

Then, he *accepted* it. He started looking for other opportunities in front of him.

Finally, he *applied* his newfound clarity by focusing on what other roles could fit his passions.

He ended up getting an opportunity to run a nonprofit medical clinic, which enriched a community that lacked many resources. He brought the incredible skills he had developed through his medical education to the work, and he helped people in ways beyond what he'd originally hoped for. This added so much joy, fulfillment, and meaning to his journey. Today, he looks back and sees that God was involved every step of the way. He believes he had to go through all he did in order to experience the good on the other side, and that humility was the hidden piece essential to getting there.

Humility empowered my friend to accept what he was not able to achieve and to do the good works God had for him. It also enabled him to celebrate the success of others authentically and not be threatened by them.

A perspective shift changed everything for him.

And this same perspective shift—along with all the new choices and possibilities it can open up—is available to you too.

Are you ready to try out some new possibilities?

CHAPTER 9

CULTIVATE IT (BEGIN THE PRACTICE)

CHICKEN TIKKA MASALA, butter chicken, lamb rogan josh, palak paneer, chana masala, aloo gobi—are you familiar with these world treasures? If you aren't, trust me, you need to get on that. They're some of my all-time favorite Indian dishes, full of rich, complex flavors and velvety creaminess. So good.

There's one ingredient that's used in each of these dishes: the curry plant. It's actually used to create the base of the majority of vegetable and meat curries in India.

Years ago my uncle Calvin, who lives in Houston and owns an Indian restaurant called Palette Indian Kitchen, planted a curry seed from India and grew a big ol' strong tree. It produced more seeds and spices, which multiplied, so he began giving family members starter curry trees. At one Thanksgiving in Houston, it was my turn. Uncle Calvin gave me two starter curry trees, along with precise instructions about how to care for them, involving a specific watering schedule and particular climate conditions.

Now, I've never been a gardener. I don't have a green thumb; I have whatever is the opposite of that. But I was determined to keep these very special plants alive.

We drove the two curry plants eighteen hours from Houston all the way home to Charlotte. To my relief, they survived a minivan ride with kids walking over, around, and, I'm pretty sure, *on* them.

My uncle had told me to transfer the plants from their current bases into slightly larger ones. I had one base that was slightly larger and another that was much larger. I didn't think this would be a problem, and I put a curry tree in each one.

In the smaller base, I used soil with extra minerals. I didn't have enough of the nutrient-dense soil to put in the larger base, so I put mostly standard soil in that one.

Over the following months, the curry tree in the smaller base flourished, with new limbs sprouting out of the main shoot and numerous new leaves starting to cover them. The curry tree in the larger base was a different story. It just stayed the same. It never grew or withered. The difference between the two trees was stark. One was flourishing; one was simply surviving.

Eventually the stagnant curry tree shriveled up. No matter how much or little water I poured into it, the outcome was the same— death. From day one it had lacked the proper base and nutrients; its soil and environment had been compromised.

The flourishing curry tree, however, continued to grow and is still thriving today. It's tall and strong and has produced leaves that have flavored countless Indian dishes in our home.

The lesson I learned from this is obvious: plants need the right kind of soil and environment to thrive and flourish.

For many years, Christian thinkers have likened humility to the fertile soil in which godliness can grow.[1] Andrew Murray, a South African pastor in the 1800s, wrote, "Humility is the only soil in which virtue takes root; a lack of humility is the explanation of every defect and failure."[2] This soil analogy aligns with Scripture's teaching and can help us understand how to pursue and develop humility in our hearts.

BOTH AT THE BEGINNING
AND THROUGHOUT

In Galatians 5, the apostle Paul listed virtues often referred to as the fruit of the Spirit. Leading up to it, he described a bleak situation, a battle that happens between our flesh and our spirit: "The flesh desires what is against the Spirit, and the Spirit desires what is against the flesh; these are opposed to each other, so that you don't do what you want" (v. 17).

I feel seen. Do you feel seen?

Then, Paul brought out a game changer. He said we're not under the Law that imprisons us to the desires of the flesh. Rather, we are led by the Spirit, who produces fruit in us.

Paul used agricultural imagery to describe this theological truth, saying, "But the *fruit* of the Spirit is . . . ," then gave an epic list of virtues that create unity and harmony (v. 22).

I find it fascinating that Paul used this imagery because we're left wondering about the nature of the fruit. How is it cultivated? Where is it planted? How do we make sure the fruit is actually produced and that its quality is sustaining and pleasing?

I'm going to come back to what I said earlier: humility is the soil from which all the virtues of the Christian life grow. So I want us to read a few verses about humility and see how they connect with these fruits of the Spirit, how humility plays a foundational role in the Spirit's transformative work in us.

> HUMILITY IS THE SOIL FROM WHICH ALL THE VIRTUES OF THE CHRISTIAN LIFE GROW.

You'll notice that some of these verses include the word *humility* while others include a description or image of it.

> Adopt the same attitude as that of Christ Jesus,
> who, existing in the form of God,
> did not consider equality with God
> as something to be exploited.
> Instead he emptied himself
> by assuming the form of a servant,
> taking on the likeness of humanity.
> And when he had come as a man,
> he humbled himself by becoming obedient
> to the point of death—
> even to death on a cross. (Philippians 2:5–8)

"This one went down to his house justified rather than the other, because everyone who exalts himself will be humbled, but the one who humbles himself will be exalted." (Luke 18:14)

"Take up my yoke and learn from me, because I am lowly and humble in heart, and you will find rest for your souls. For my yoke is easy and my burden is light." (Matthew 11:29–30)

"Whoever humbles himself like this child—this one is the greatest in the kingdom of heaven." (Matthew 18:4)

"If I, your Lord and Teacher, have washed your feet, you also ought to wash one another's feet. For I have given you an example, that you also should do just as I have done for you." (John 13:14–15)

Live in harmony with one another. Do not be proud; instead, associate with the humble. Do not be wise in your own estimation. (Romans 12:16)

I, the prisoner in the Lord, urge you to walk worthy of the calling you have received, with all humility and gentleness, with patience, bearing with one another in love, making every effort to keep the unity of the Spirit through the bond of peace. (Ephesians 4:1–3)

As God's chosen people, holy and dearly loved, clothe yourselves with compassion, kindness, humility, gentleness and patience. (Colossians 3:12 NIV)

This is only the tip of the iceberg, y'all. There are so many more verses.

I find it fascinating that humility is presented both as something that starts the Christian life *and* as something included in a list of Christian virtues, as a quality we're meant to possess throughout the Christian life.

So, which one is it?

The answer is actually simple. Both.

The Christian life starts with humility. Like we've discussed, humility is what flows out of humanity when we:

- see God as he truly is;
- see ourselves in light of who God is; and
- see others as God does.

It is the result of seeing ourselves in light of who God is, which informs and shapes how we see and treat others.

We develop humility by first becoming *aware* of reality—of the greatness and grandeur of God, of our own value and worth, of the dignity of others.

Then we *accept* that the greatness and kindness of God will now change our perspective and lifestyle. For us, pride is poison and humility is life. The creation agrees with the Creator.

Then we "*adopt* the same attitude as that of Christ Jesus" (Philippians 2:5). In the power of the Holy Spirit, we live out humility day after day.

This is what we're after.

If we don't do all three parts, it's like trying to grow a plant apart from soil. We'll never experience true humility and the gifts and virtues connected to it. Picture fertile soil forever separated from a seed. It is a waste of excellent soil waiting to produce something healthy and good. And it's a tragedy for the seed that stays in a state of immaturity, never developing into what it could and should be. The soil and the seed need each other in order to begin the growth process.

And if we have humility only at the beginning of our faith, it's like yanking a thriving plant out of its soil. The rest of our Christian life will suffer. Just as the missing soil is the explanation for a dying plant, our "lack of humility," in Murray's words, "is the explanation of every defect and failure."[3]

CULTIVATING = BECOMING AND PRACTICING

When we adopt humility, the same attitude of Jesus, we're taking his approach to life. We're saying yes to transformation, welcoming the Spirit to shape us into the image of Christ.

Where in the world do we start?

By recognizing Jesus' own humility as he entered into humanity. Theologians refer to this miraculous moment in history as the *incarnation*.

Jesus gave us a powerful picture of humility by washing the disciples' feet. When we picture this, it's easy to envision our sorta-grubby feet in a bubbly soak, like when we go get a mani-pedi. Yes—moment of honesty—Britt and I do this, and, yes, it's become our go-to date thing. It actually took a few years of Britt trying to convince me to give it a shot. The first time I went, I panicked when I realized I had to take my socks off and put my feet in water and that people would be working on my toes with tools that seemed to come from a medieval torture tool kit. I've slowly gotten over it. And I always tip them well because, y'all, feet can get gross.

Let me tell you, feet washing in the ancient world was even nastier. It was common for feet to be caked with not only dirt but also garbage, dung, urine—lots of repulsive stuff—after walking those ancient streets. Jesus, God in the flesh, got on bended knee to wash *those* kinds of feet.

This act of humility was one of many for Jesus, all intended to reveal his nature. It continued a pattern of humble acts and pointed to what was coming next in his story. If the disciples had been looking closely, they'd have seen the incarnation, a ministry of selfless service, feet washing . . . and then the crucifixion.

The cross, the ultimate symbol of humility, defeat, and weakness, is where Jesus' earthly life ended and where our Christian life begins. Death was not an end for Jesus; it was something he entered into and went through in order to reach new life. And we get to join him in that. We get to join Christ in his death, burial, and resurrection in order to live his life of humility on earth.

This means that humility truly is a fundamental aspect of life with Jesus. As we're united with him, it's the oxygen we breathe. It's the clothing we're always wearing. It's the soil we're rooted in. We *become* a humble person, just like he was.

This also means that humility should be the fragrance that marks every Christian virtue.

> HUMILITY SHOULD BE THE FRAGRANCE THAT MARKS EVERY CHRISTIAN VIRTUE.

Let's go back to that list of virtues (fruit) in Galatians 5:22–24. I'm going to paraphrase the list a bit to account for the soil of humility that is necessary for the fruit of the Spirit, to help us think about how humility relates to each one.

The fruit of the Spirit is

- love that was extended to us by the humble act of a gracious God;
- joy that is placed within our hearts to praise God (because humility makes us aware of the goodness of God);
- peace that is established in our lives when we humbly see each other in light of the cross of Jesus;
- patience that is practiced because we are humbly aware of the patience of God in our own lives;
- kindness that flows from us because of the humble kindness of God that flowed to us in Christ;
- goodness that marks our lives because in humility we know the only one who is truly good is God;
- faithfulness as evidence of humble commitment because we have experienced the unfailing faithfulness of God;
- gentleness as the default humble posture of the believer because we've seen the pattern of gentleness Jesus had with those on the margins of society; and
- self-control exercised because we're humbly aware of the work of the Spirit to restrain us, equip us, and empower us.

As the fruits of the Spirit grow out of the soil of humility, each one is laced with the fragrance of humility. We start with humility.

And then we are sustained, equipped, and empowered *through a constant practice of returning to humility.*

This is cultivating humility. It's an ongoing pursuit, even as it becomes more and more ingrained in us.

WHEN HUMILITY IS ABSENT

There are a couple of stories in the New Testament that can help this idea sink in for us. They are the stories of Zechariah, the father of John the Baptist, and of Mary, the mother of Jesus (Luke 1:5–56). We're going to look at both of them through the lens of humility.

Let's begin with the meaning of the name *Zechariah*, which is, "Yahweh remembers." This meaning is significant for Zechariah's story in both a societal and personal way.

Societally, the Jewish people were under the subjection of a foreign enemy, Rome. The Israelite people longed for God to remember them and rescue them. They were in a position of weakness and needed the strength of God. Zechariah and his wife, Elizabeth, were both considered righteous and blameless, yet they had no children. I'm sure Zechariah wondered if God actually remembered his people, the Israelites, and him personally.

God sent the angel Gabriel to tell Zechariah and Elizabeth that they would conceive and have a child. He specifically said that Zechariah's prayers had been heard. That *God had remembered!*

Did Zechariah respond with whoops of celebration?

No. He immediately questioned how this could be possible because both he and his wife were advanced in years.

Zechariah's response is intriguing, and really, not something I can blame him for. I think Zechariah just had an extra dose of realism and logic. The only problem is, he should have realized that reason and logic get thrown out the window when an angel of God is standing before you, speaking a message from God himself. The consequence for Zechariah's unbelief was that his mouth was shut. He was subjected to silence.

Now, here's something else you need to know about Zechariah: he was a priest of God who held position, status, and a certain amount of power. Losing the ability to speak would be difficult for anyone, but for someone who was used to being in a position of authority, it must have felt like a real shock to the system. It also was a pretty significant blow to his role as a priest, relying on his voice for his vocation!

Here's what we have in Zechariah's situation: a person who had power, status, and privilege, who needed to be reminded that when God speaks, we should not only listen; we need to *believe*. Zechariah was struck with silence as a symbol of humility.

WHEN HUMILITY IS PRESENT

A few verses later we see the angel Gabriel visit Mary, the mother of Jesus, to inform her that the Holy Spirit would come upon her and she would conceive and give birth to Jesus.

Mary was, of course, a young woman betrothed to marriage but not yet married. Women in the ancient world did not necessarily have power, position, or privilege, and if they did, it was typically through marriage and family resources. With Mary there was no indication of these things. In the world's eyes, she was unimpressive, not proving herself special or remarkable in any way. In fact, Mary acknowledged this herself, saying, "He has looked on the humble [*tapeinōsin*] estate of his servant. For behold, from now on all generations will call me blessed" (Luke 1:48 ESV).

Everything about this story leaves us scratching our heads.

Why didn't God go after a princess or a woman of royalty? Why this Galilean virgin, Mary?

But wait. This is a pattern for God, isn't it? Remember, patterns have a purpose!

First Corinthians 1 tells us, "God chose the foolish things of the world to shame the wise; God chose the weak things of the world to shame the strong. God chose the lowly things of this world and the despised things—and the things that are not—to nullify the things that are" (vv. 27–28 NIV).

It's a good reminder for us that God's routine is to use surprising things, people, and situations to show us his kindness and power. God chose Mary, a woman, a virgin, someone of true humility, and exalted her.

Mary questioned Gabriel, but she did it in a different way than Zechariah did.

"How can this be, since I have not had sexual relations with a man?" she asked (Luke 1:34).

Her question wasn't motivated by doubt, like Zechariah's was (even though he should have known better, being a priest and knowing the stories of Abraham, Sarah, and Hannah). It was more about biology. Literally, this was a miraculous conception. There is innocence in her question, and it's comforting to know we can ask God questions like this.

Gabriel explained that the Holy Spirit would create this life in her. "Nothing will be impossible with God," he said (v. 37).

When Mary heard this, she believed.

"See, I am the Lord's servant," she said. "May it happen to me as you have said" (v. 38).

Later, when Mary was visiting Elizabeth (Zechariah's wife), baby John leaped for joy in Elizabeth's womb. And Mary broke out into a song of praise (vv. 39–56)!

Okay, let's just pause and take a quick account of where we are.

> HUMILITY IS FOR
> ALL PEOPLE IN ALL
> PLACES, REGARDLESS
> OF SITUATION OR
> CIRCUMSTANCE.

Zechariah the priest—a man; a person of power, position, and privilege[4]—was silenced so he could cultivate humility in his life.

Mary—a woman; a virgin; someone with no power, position, or privilege—broke out into a song of praise as a result of having cultivated humility in her life.

Humility is for all people in all places, regardless of situation or circumstance.

PRAISING FROM A POSTURE OF HUMILITY

Mary's song is really important, so let's take a look at that.

It's often referred to as "the Magnificat," which comes from the first word of the Latin translation, *Magnificat anima mea Dominum*, meaning "My soul magnifies the Lord." The song itself is poetic and has similarities with various Hebrew songs and poetry found in Psalms and elsewhere in the Old Testament. It especially resembles Hannah's song in 1 Samuel 2:1–10. Hannah was also a woman, barren, and responded in praise from a posture of humility.

Here's how Mary's song reads:

> My soul magnifies the Lord,
> and my spirit rejoices in God my Savior,
> because he has looked with favor
> on the humble condition of his servant.
> Surely, from now on all generations
> will call me blessed,

because the Mighty One
has done great things for me,
and his name is holy.
His mercy is from generation to generation
on those who fear him.
He has done a mighty deed with his arm;
he has scattered the proud
because of the thoughts of their hearts;
he has toppled the mighty from their thrones
and exalted the lowly.
He has satisfied the hungry with good things
and sent the rich away empty.
He has helped his servant Israel,
remembering his mercy
to Abraham and his descendants forever,
just as he spoke to our ancestors.

(Luke 1:46–55)

Mary's song can be broken down into four parts:[5]

1. Rejoicing (vv. 46–48)

    Mary acknowledged the honor and privilege it would be to give birth to the long-awaited Messiah. This reflects Mary's awareness of God and his kindness.
2. Glorifying (vv. 49–50)

    Mary glorified and exalted God for his might, holiness, and mercy. This is further indication of her awareness of God.
3. Anticipating (vv. 51–53)

    Mary said she was waiting for the day when Jesus the Messiah would transform and conform the world, when he would pull down the proud and exalt the humble.

4. Exalting (vv. 54–55)

Mary lifted up the name of God for his past covenant faithfulness and his present faithfulness, which gave her assurance of his future faithfulness.

Mary's song was informed by the humility she'd cultivated in her life, in her given context. It seems almost impossible to rejoice in God, glorify him for his greatness, anticipate his continued goodness, and exalt him for his faithfulness *without* a deep-rooted humility.

When we look at these two stories, we can see the importance of living out the fruit of humility in our lives. In Zechariah's case the silence was that reminder. In Mary's case the song of praise was a response. I have a suspicion that Mary reflected on that song as the years went on. I also believe that Zechariah held on to that time of silence as a reminder of God's patience.

It seems humility was necessary for both Zechariah and Mary. Why? Some may say it was required for that moment, the miraculous birth of two baby boys: one Jesus called the greatest prophet to ever live; the other, God in the flesh. But I think there was more to this.

The necessity for a cultivated humility was also in preparation for later parts of their stories. Zechariah and Elizabeth would celebrate the success and greatness of John the Baptist's ministry and endure his tragic death. Mary and Joseph could take captive in their hearts every moment and miracle of Jesus the Messiah's life. And Mary could recall those moments in the most humbling moment in human history—when her Son, the Savior of the world, endured death on a cross.

This is why we need humility today. And it's why humility isn't something we can simply win at, achieve, and move on from. Humility needs to be the soil of our Christian lives that we tend to, cultivate, and return to consistently. It needs to *become a part of us.* Then it can equip us for today and teach us how to endure whatever comes our way tomorrow.

What if today we made it our conviction and commitment to sing our own "song of humility"? Now, don't panic. I'm not going to ask you to step out in the halls of your workplace, your school, or the mall and do your best *Sound of Music* (or *High School Musical*) impression. But I am going to ask you what it may look like to pause and write in your journal (or Notes app) a simple "song" of remembrance that you could use to remind yourself of how important it is to practice a lifestyle of humility.

> HUMILITY NEEDS TO BE THE SOIL OF OUR CHRISTIAN LIVES THAT WE TEND TO, CULTIVATE, AND RETURN TO CONSISTENTLY.

Good news: Mary gave us the framework for our very own song.

1. *Rejoice in the greatness of God.*

   Write down two or three things that remind you how big God is. For me, it's the stars, the ocean, and the landscape of a shrinking world as I'm taking off in a plane and flying into the clouds.

2. *Glorify God.*

   Take those two or three things and write out a simple prayer of praise. Allow thankfulness in your heart to turn into praise on your lips.

3. *Anticipate God's continual faithfulness.*

   Our story is a little different from Mary's. She looked forward to the day the Messiah would bring rescue. You and I look back to the cross and remember that the symbol of ultimate defeat was flipped to the symbol of total victory. He's been so good to us, and we can be sure that he will keep on being good to us. Write about a specific way he's been faithful to you and how you know he will be just as faithful in the future.

4. *Exalt God.*

The empty grave is the assurance of God's promise fulfilled and a reminder that he always follows through on his promises. Anytime you have a doubt, remember that the grave is empty and has stayed empty. All the Romans had to do to disprove this whole thing was show the people a body, and they never were able to! Today we can exalt God because he never changes and his power and goodness will never end. We exalt God because he is the only one worthy of exaltation. Write a line or two to express this.

As we sing our own song that reminds us of God's steadfast love and faithfulness, we are living and embodying the humble life.

As we've said, to cultivate humility is to practice it. There is no one greater who practiced and embodied the life of humility than Jesus himself.

Let's start learning all we can from him.

120

CHAPTER 10

EMBODY IT (LIKE JESUS)

I KNOW I'M biased, but I think I grew up in one of the best eras in human history. I got to watch multiple technology explosions change the way we do life, from brick-sized cell phones to handheld computer–type smartphones; from the slow, noisy DSL dial-up internet to ultraspeedy fiber internet; from tiny cube TVs with, like, four superblurry channels to flat monstrosities with lifelike picture quality.

But none of these things is what makes my era especially awesome. It's the fact that I grew up in the early '90s heyday of Chicago. All I need to say is two words: *Michael Jordan*.

Every weekend was a party with my family and friends as we met up at different houses to catch the Bulls game. Playoffs were totally magical. Jordan kept doing the unexplainable. The way he jumped and moved with the ball in the air? It truly was greatness.

I watched MJ lead the Bulls to their first three-peat (winning three championships in a row). I cried when MJ announced his retirement. I sobbed uncontrollably when he announced he was playing baseball and then kept sobbing watching him play baseball. When he spoke the words "I'm back" before going on to lead the Bulls to *another* three-peat, my tears of sorrow turned into tears of joy!

Nike's slogan "Just do it" was good, but "Be like Mike" was next-level. I desperately wanted to be like Mike. To jump like him. To shoot like him. To wear his iconic number, 23, on my jersey. MJ was a generation's role model and ambition. And you better believe I've carried this into adulthood. Our daughter Emelia Jane's nickname, EmJ, is a throwback to the greatest to ever play basketball!

If you're thinking, *But what about LeBron James?* I have a simple response: Whose number did LeBron start with in his career? *23.* That's right. End of discussion.

Long before MJ's slogan "Be like Mike," there was a different "slogan" that the first followers of Jesus used. The name they gave themselves and their shared approach to life was simply "the Way."[1] It was a reference to following the life and ways of Jesus the Messiah, who was crucified on a cross and who defeated death through death.

It's the same "Jesus way of life" we want to learn and live out. So we're going to look at some verses that will give us more insight into "the Way," looking at both the words of Jesus and the words of Paul.

THE LIGHTER WAY

Jesus said to his disciples, "Take up My yoke and learn from Me, because I am gentle and humble in heart, and you will find rest for yourselves. For My yoke is easy and My burden is light" (Matthew 11:29–30 HCSB).

In this invitation to exchange yokes, Jesus was contrasting his way of life with the religious leaders' way of life. His way was light. Their way for God's people was weighed down by a load of extra rules, which had become a seriously heavy burden for the people. This was great for the leaders, who used those rules to maintain authority, but it was defeating for the people, who had to live up to those expectations.

My kids would tell you that this has been their experience in our home. No, Britt and I have not broken child labor laws—though you might think so if you listened to them. Their chores have simply increased in proportion to their age; they are capable of more now, so they have to do more to help around the house.

One day, my boys decided to sit their mom and me down for a "family talk."

They said that it was unfair of us to expect them to do so many chores. They were kids, and they should be having fun.

I took a deep breath (which often grounds me and, in a very real way, can keep me from sinning in trying parenting moments!). Then I explained to them that doing chores in the house was important, and that we were training them for the future. I also compared it to discipleship and said it's what Jesus wants from all of us.

They were unimpressed and unconvinced by my answer.

Then Britt jumped in. "Well, at least the three of you can share the load of work together! Imagine if you had to do it by yourself."

I didn't expect this comment from my wife to make any kind of impact. But six little brown eyes got big. They looked at each other and whispered, "Yeah, what if we had to do it all on our own? Maybe we should stop talking about this. They could make us do it by ourselves."

They looked at Britt and me and said, "Thanks, Mom and Dad. We're good." And they walked off.

I'll be honest. I was a little salty. I mean, I made a great connection to our faith and the Bible, and these boys couldn't have cared less. Then my wife made one small comment, and it changed their whole perspective?

There was something significant in her words that I overlooked though: the thought that the burden is not lonely but shared. The reality of the fun that takes place in working alongside someone you love and care about. All of this matters.

Let's just hold on to that as we get back to Matthew 11.

Jesus told his disciples to "take up [his] yoke" and learn from him (v. 29).

The rabbis often spoke of the "yoke of Law" in a loving and favorable way,[2] which makes sense since they were the ones in authority. The Law was something they used to remind the people of their inability and how they needed to do better and be better. So the everyday person would have felt like the "yoke of the Law" was unbearable, even cruel.

Now, you may be thinking this is a back-then problem with no modern-day version. But I'm dealing with rules every day that seem to be overkill, and you may be also. It's when the voice of comparison tells me the only way to be happy is to have the same size house as my friend or upgrade my car to match my neighbors. Or when my Instagram feed tells me my body size and shape isn't good enough and the only way to gain health and acceptance is by looking a certain way. Or when my wife requires our family to transition from regular rice to cauliflower rice. (Y'all, I'm Indian. This is a painful thing that has been placed on me.) Jokes aside, you get the point. We are dealing with similar issues today, and Jesus' message about his different yoke applies to us.

His reference to the yoke could be either a human yoke, which was placed on the shoulders of a person to balance the weight and lessen the strain on the body, or an animal yoke, which connected two animals to pull the burden together.

I think the imagery here is rich and beautiful for a few reasons. First, because God in his kindness never desires his children to be crushed by an unbearable weight. This is why he gives us a yoke.

Further, the yoke is bearable because Jesus himself carries the burden with us and, in fact, front-loads it. While it's impossible for us to truly take on "the yoke of the Law"—to follow the Law completely—Jesus does so perfectly.[3]

THE GENTLE AND HUMBLE WAY

In joining Jesus and being yoked with him, we are learning from the Teacher himself. In the phrase "learn from me" in Matthew 11:29, the Greek word translated as "learn" (*mathete*) is associated with the meaning of "discipling." Jesus calls us to a type of learning rooted in discipleship through instruction.[4] And he teaches us in practical ways.

Jesus wants us to learn from him because he is both gentle and humble. In the English Standard Version, the Greek word translated as "gentle" in verse 29 (*praus*) refers to "freedom from pretension (1 Peter 3:14–15), gentleness (Matthew 11:29; James 3:13), and patient endurance of injury—where it is proper to endure."[5] Jesus is free from and rejects any type of pretension. He dealt with people in gentleness when appropriate (the woman at the well in John 4) and endured injury when it was proper (the cross).

Jesus also described himself as humble. We'll spend more time with the Greek word translated as "humble" here (*tapeinos*) in the next chapter. For now it's important to note that, in the Greco-Roman world, this word had an almost universally negative connotation. It dealt with lowliness or subservience. No one had any sort of positive way to think of these things. No one desired to have any version of them in their lives.

GENTLE HUMILITY IN THE LIFE OF JESUS WAS A WILLINGNESS TO BE LOW AND TO CONSIDER OTHERS.

But here, Jesus connected it to a lowliness of heart. Gentle humility in the life of Jesus was a willingness to be low and to consider others. This was deeply rooted in his heart and at the core of who he was. I would go so far as to say that humility shaped and influenced his gentleness. It was also the backdrop of his greatness.

This is what Jesus calls us to. He invites us to come share his yoke—there's room for us there—to walk right beside him, learning his ways of gentleness and humility. The blessing in this is that we will not be crushed. We will experience a "perfect fit" because Jesus promises to carry anything and everything that is beyond what we can bear.

It's important to point out that this is an exchange of yokes, not a *removal* of yokes.

We still carry burdens; we still have to walk through our fears and navigate the hurts of life. But the yoke of Jesus removes the crushing weight of fear and pain for something that is a good fit for our shoulders so we can walk through the hurts of life and make it to the other side.

And friends, when we experience this good fit, we are set up for the peace that God desires for our lives. We are equipped with the confidence that our souls long for because Jesus is right beside us.

THE "NEVER ALONE" WAY

Maybe the unexpected beauty and blessing here is that, as we take up our yoke, we can look next to us and see Jesus. The same way my oldest son, Liam, washes dishes and looks to his right and sees his younger brother Levi drying dishes. Or when Levi looks up from the dishes he's drying and sees his younger brother, Luke, wiping down the tables. Then Luke looks around and sees his little baby sister, EmJ, watching all three of them doing chores and gets comfort as he thinks, *Soon, you're going to join us in this.* There is a joy in their hearts because they bear their burdens together. They tell jokes and catch up on the school day and work through the burden of their chores together. Their joint presence makes it not only bearable but unexpectedly enjoyable.

When we look over and see Jesus by our side, it is the unexpected joy of his presence that gets us through the hard parts of the day. It is the presence of Jesus that gives us courage to face the pain of today and tomorrow. Sometimes, we just need to remind ourselves to look to our right and smile as we feel his steady, gentle, humble, and strong presence walking alongside us.

Jesus promises us one of the greatest gifts we could ask for, and that's rest. The rest he gives doesn't remove the burdens we experience; it makes it possible to carry them well.

Jesus said that if we take on his yoke and adopt his way of living, we will find rest for our souls. In other words, the hidden piece in life we've been longing for—to experience peace—is humility.

THE HUMBLE OBEDIENCE WAY

Now we're going to turn to Paul's words about Jesus in Philippians 2. It's a passage we talked about already, but because it's a key passage about Jesus' humility, we're going to look at it again more closely.

> Adopt the same attitude as that of Christ Jesus,
> who, existing in the form of God,
> did not consider equality with God
> as something to be exploited.

> Instead he emptied himself
> by assuming the form of a servant,
> taking on the likeness of humanity.
> And when he had come as a man,
> he humbled himself by becoming obedient
> to the point of death—
> even to death on a cross. (vv. 5–8)

This is an immense theological truth. This is where you insert the mind-blown emoji.

Paul described the fact that God became man without losing an ounce of his divinity, that he took on human flesh in an act of ultimate humility. Remember, theologians refer to this as the *incarnation*.

Andrew Murray described it this way:

> What is the Incarnation but His heavenly humility, His emptying himself and becoming man? What is His life on earth but humility; His taking the form of a servant? And what is His atonement but humility? "He humbled himself and became obedient to death." And what is His ascension and His glory but humility exalted to the throne and crowned with glory? "He humbled himself . . . therefore God exalted Him to the highest place."[6]

I love the phrase "heavenly humility" in reference to the incarnation. If we've ever feared that God doesn't really love us, the incarnation is proof he does. We can repeatedly turn to it and be reminded over and over of his massive, outrageous love for us. Jesus is God in humble flesh and an expression of eternal love.

Paul included some key phrases in these verses that I don't want us to miss. I have them circled in my Bible. Let's walk through them together.

EMBODY IT (LIKE JESUS)

"ADOPT THE SAME ATTITUDE AS THAT OF CHRIST JESUS"

This is the ancient version of "Be like Mike," but instead we could rephrase it as "Be like Jesus."

The word *adopt* is telling us to take purposeful action toward becoming something we currently are not. It also leaves us with a sense of responsibility. It's up to us to decide to join Jesus on the journey of humility.

I have some close friends who have walked through the adoption process. They decided to bring a child who was not part of their biological family into an intimate relationship. To adopt that child was to give them the place, the love, and the opportunity a biological child would have. It was an act of love, and, of course, it involved a cost.

Adopting the attitude of Jesus is a decision we get to make out of love. It comes with a cost, but the blessing and benefit is so worth it.

"HE HUMBLED HIMSELF BY BECOMING OBEDIENT TO THE POINT OF DEATH"

Jesus, who is God, took on human flesh. This is really important because it makes humility possible for Jesus. If he were not truly human, he would have no humility to exercise. It would be like playing a game that is rigged. It would be unfair, and the win would be meaningless.

So Jesus took on humanity, adding it to his divinity. And in his earthly life, he modeled servanthood, which ultimately led him to death on the cross. Some scholars refer to this concept as "divine humility."[7]

An incredible example of this is Luke 22:42, when Jesus, hours before heading to the cross, prayed, "Father, if you are willing, remove this cup from me. Nevertheless, not my will, but yours, be done" (ESV). Jesus was fully aware of who the Father was. Because he knew who the Father was, he intimately understood his role and responsibility as the Son. Because he knew who he was and where the Father was leading him, he understood his path was the way of the cross.[8]

But of course this wasn't the end of the story. That darkest day in human history brought the beginning of a new hope for all of humanity—all because of the overwhelming love of God and the humble obedience of Jesus his Son.

"FOR THIS REASON"

The book of Philippians says,

> For this reason God highly exalted him
> and gave him the name
> that is above every name,
> so that at the name of Jesus
> every knee will bow—
> in heaven and on earth
> and under the earth—
> and every tongue will confess
> that Jesus Christ is Lord,
> to the glory of God the Father. (2:9–11)

For this reason! Because of the humility Jesus displayed on the cross, he was exalted and given authority!

On the cross Jesus was lifted up and elevated high for everyone to see and to witness his total defeat. In a way, the Romans built a ladder for Jesus to climb up so the world would know that he was no true king and that Rome was still in charge. Caesar, the Romans, and the enemies of our souls, the devil and his evil supernatural beings, had no clue they'd built a ladder that would eventually lead to Jesus' enthronement. Jesus' humble obedience—his willingness to go through the journey of the cross—resulted in his elevation as the reigning King of the world.

We build ladders to climb so we can reach things up high, like when we hang Christmas lights on a roof's edge. But the largest ladder in the world wouldn't get us near the stars—and not just because they're higher than the ladder but because no ladder could do the job. Even with the most powerful rocket in existence, we'd still lack the means to reach those stars.

In a similar way, knowing God and being known by God was not simply out of reach for us after the fall in Genesis 3; it was *impossible* through our own means. The humility of Jesus on the cross reversed what was impossible and created the possibility for us to truly know God.

HUMILITY ROUTINES

Okay, so we now have a better idea of how Jesus embodied humility. While we won't be able to do it perfectly, like he did, we can learn as much as we can from him and follow after him. We begin by asking, How was Jesus able to live in such constant humility? How was he able to act out in perfect obedience? The secret for Jesus was a constant return to the Father.

Earlier we looked at how Jesus prayed and submitted his desires in humble obedience to the Father. But this wasn't the first time Jesus was in conversation with the Father. In fact, there was something specific Jesus did repeatedly to ensure this connection: he withdrew to lonely or deserted places.

Jesus had a principle and pattern of solitude, a time and space set aside for prayer and meditation. Sometimes he did this on his own; other times he invited his closest friends.

Consider these passages:

- Luke 9:10: Jesus went away with his disciples to be in a lonely place by themselves.
- Matthew 14:13: Jesus withdrew to a lonely place.
- Mark 1:35: Jesus went out to a lonely place and prayed.
- John 6:15: Jesus withdrew into the hills by himself.
- Mark 6:31: Jesus went out to a lonely place and rested.

One of the most practical things you can do to foster a lifestyle of humility is invest in your personal emotional, physical, and spiritual health.

Think about it: Jesus repeatedly withdrew to lonely places, and a bunch of those times he walked up a hill (physical). Other times he rested (emotional). And other times he prayed (spiritual). He nurtured and cared for every part of his humanity (physical, emotional, spiritual) during these times of solitude.

> ONE OF THE MOST PRACTICAL THINGS YOU CAN DO TO FOSTER A LIFESTYLE OF HUMILITY IS INVEST IN YOUR PERSONAL EMOTIONAL, PHYSICAL, AND SPIRITUAL HEALTH.

Today is a great day to build some time into your schedule to sneak away and begin to construct some routines of humility. For Jesus it was prayer, walks, solitude, and rest. The same could be true for us.

Here are a few things you can do to start your humility routine:[9]

1. Thank God. Find a reason, hopefully many reasons, to be grateful for his kindness and provision in your life.
2. Be honest about your weaknesses, limits, and inability. Confess these things to God and ask him for help.

3. Prepare yourself for things to go sideways. Make a pre-commitment that whether you experience success or humiliation, you will remain grounded. Learn to accept ups and downs and commit always to move forward.

4. Laugh early and laugh often. Make it a practice to find fun so you can avoid taking yourself too seriously and constantly thinking of your troubles. It's honestly a way to care for your soul.

As we follow Jesus and his path of humility, we can be assured that what is true of him will be true for us. Humility grounded Jesus, and the Father lifted him high.

This is what we have to look forward to.

Scholars refer to this way of living as *cruciformity*.[10] I like to think of it simply as the "Jesus way of life"—the lighter, more gentle and humble, "never alone" way. The way Jesus lived out and invites us into with him.

"Come to me," he says to you now. How do you want to respond?

CHAPTER 11

REDEFINE IT (LIKE PAUL)

I HAD ONLY just met this dude and already could tell he was category-one friend material.

Yeah, I've got friend categories. You've got them too, I'm sure. Mine go like this:

1. The friend who is ride or die. You can hang out at any time, and it takes absolutely no work.
2. The friend who is awesome but best enjoyed with a group. There can be awkward moments of silence if you are alone, so it's better to keep a third person close by, just in case the conversation needs some help.
3. The friend who is great to hang out with once in a while. There is a connection, but it's not deep, and that's okay.

Well, I'd just met this new friend at a conference. When we realized we were both trying to figure out how to sneak away to watch the NBA finals, we bonded over having the right priorities.

So together we found a restaurant showing the game and kept each other company.

We were getting along super well, having fun. But then he started saying some pretty disturbing stuff. I started rethinking the whole "category one" thing.

"Man, iPhones are overrated," he told me. "They're so expensive, you can only use one kind of charger with them, and they lock you into the whole Apple system. Androids are where it's at. They've got way more customization, compatibility, and storage options."

What?! This was *unbelievable*—basically heresy in my book!

Then things got much worse.

A few minutes later, he uttered the words, "I know everybody goes nuts over Michael Jordan, but seriously, LeBron James is incredible. He deserves the title of the greatest basketball player of all time—like, by a long shot." I'll be honest, the peace we had was absolutely threatened!

This was, without a doubt, *the most shocking thing he could have said to me.* Could I even stay in the restaurant with him now?

I did stay. And while I didn't exactly keep my cool, I wasn't rude as I set him straight. I fought for the honorable GOAT status to remain squarely with the legendary MJ. Where it belongs.

Against all odds, this guy and I found a way to push past these massive divisions in our beliefs and even stayed in touch. Today we are full-on category-one friends. Whenever I see that green bubble text message from him, my heart still aches a bit for him (the lost soul!), but I always respond (after saying a short prayer for him), which is yet another sign in this world that the gospel unites very different people.

Yeah, so, I've got my strong convictions about technology and sports. I'm sure you've got your own strong convictions too. Think back to the last time you heard someone say something and your instant reaction was, *Did she just say that?!* Or, *Oh no, he did not go there!*

There are relatively few things everyone would wholeheartedly agree on today. In the ancient Greco-Roman world, however, there were certain things everyone saw the same way. Their culture had an *anthropocentric* view of humanity, which basically means they had a *human-centered* lens. They formed all their basic beliefs about the world, about what was good and bad, through the lens of humanity.

This shaped their understanding of humility. They saw it as something that constricted human rights and prevented freedom—and anything that compromised or restricted freedom was despised.[1] I won't say humility was their version of "LeBron James is the greatest" exactly, but you get the idea. They were seriously against humility.

This was Paul's cultural context when he wrote about humility—and he wrote about it a lot. We're going to look at what he said about it so we can get a glimpse of how the humility of Christians was disruptive (in the best way) back then, which will help us see how powerful it can be for us today. Yes, Paul's world was much different from ours, but in some foundational ways it was also similar. If we can grasp those similarities, we'll be able to see how humility is the key to experiencing peace today, not someday.

AN ANCIENT CULTURAL SHAKE-UP

First, let's look at how the Greek word for *humility* was used in Paul's setting. One of the prominent Greek words we translate as "humble" (*tapeinophrosynē*) could also be translated as "self-abasement" or "lowliness." In Greek, words related to each other that convey the concept of humility are referred to as "word groups." Markus Barth, a renowned Swiss New Testament scholar who lived during the second half of the 1900s, shared this insight about the *humility* word group: "The entire word group which belongs with *tapeinophrosynē*, according to its usage in common Greek, is used in a negative sense and means a low slavish orientation."[2]

This means the concept of humility would have been something totally shameful.[3] The culture was highly competitive and focused on self-exaltation (sounds familiar, doesn't it?). So anyone who had low social status, who was weak or lowly, was considered "humble," and it almost always had a negative connotation.[4]

Let's step back to process what this means. Imagine walking into an ancient coffee shop in the Greco-Roman world. You see groups of people sipping their favorite specialty coffee drinks. You step up to the coffee bar, place your order, then walk to the area where you will get your drink.

Then, someone walks into the coffee shop and the entire place goes quiet. People begin whispering. "I know that guy. He's *humble.*" The entire atmosphere changes. People's faces turn from pleasant to disgusted. Every time this new person gets near someone else, they move away from him. No one speaks to him or even looks at him. He is considered an outsider, a social reject. If you got near him or talked to him, you would be included in that severe judgment, so it would be best to stay far, far away.

This was how humility was understood in the ancient world. The early church father Augustine went so far as to say humility was an unknown virtue in the ancient world.[5] Given this cultural climate, imagine how shocking and disruptive it was when Paul told the church in Rome, "Live in harmony with one another. Do not be proud; instead, associate with the *humble* [*tapeinos*]. Do not be wise in your own estimation" (Romans 12:16). There had to have been some jaws on the floor. I can picture people sliding out the door of that house church thinking, *These people have lost their minds. Ain't nobody got time for dat.*

This isn't the only time Paul said something like this. It was a consistent theme throughout his letters—he taught it to the churches in Rome, Corinth, Ephesus, Philippi, and Colossae.

> When we came into Macedonia, we had no rest. Instead, we were troubled in every way: conflicts on the outside, fears within. But God, who comforts the *downcast* [*tapeinos*], comforted us by the arrival of Titus. (2 Corinthians 7:5–6)

> I, the prisoner in the Lord, urge you to walk worthy of the calling you have received, with all *humility* [*tapeinophrosynē*] and gentleness, with patience, bearing with one another in love, making every effort to keep the unity of the Spirit through the bond of peace. (Ephesians 4:1–3)

> Do nothing out of selfish ambition or conceit, but in *humility* [*tapeinophrosynē*] consider others as more important than yourselves. Everyone should look not to his own interests, but rather to the interests of others. (Philippians 2:3–4)

> As God's chosen ones, holy and dearly loved, put on compassion, kindness, *humility* [*tapeinophrosynē*], gentleness, and patience. (Colossians 3:12)

> He will transform the body of our *humble* [*tapeinōseōs*] condition into the likeness of his glorious body, by the power that enables him to subject everything to himself. (Philippians 3:21)

Over and over, Paul reiterated the importance of the humble life for the believer in Jesus.

When the people sitting in these churches first heard these words from Paul, they might have thought, *Wait a minute. Did Paul really say the H-* [I guess in Greek, the *T-*] *word?* He presented it as the identity-forming virtue that should mark Christians. What motivated Paul to make such a countercultural, even offensive, claim?

It's actually pretty simple. He followed the Messiah, Jesus, who lived a countercultural life that was offensive to both the Romans and the religious elite.

Paul's most striking use of humility might be in Philippians 2:8–9: "He [Jesus] *humbled* [*tapeinōsen*] himself by becoming obedient to the point of death—even to death on a cross. For this reason God highly exalted him and gave him the name that is above every name."

Because we find ourselves "in Christ" (another favorite saying of Paul: Romans 8:1; 1 Corinthians 1:30; Galatians 2:16), it makes sense for us to identify ourselves with him in all things, especially in his humility. Why? Because the very thing that was true of Jesus will be true of us. Jesus humbled himself, and his humility led him through humiliation—but humiliation was not the end for him. As we've seen, humility was his path of exaltation.

This unity with him and shared exaltation with him is exactly what we just saw in Philippians 3:21: "He will transform the body of our humble condition into the likeness of his glorious body." What was true of Jesus will be true of us.

A KINGDOM VIEW OF HUMILITY

Do you desire exaltation? Scripture leaves no doubt about it: the path to being lifted high begins with going low. It begins with living out humility.

There's more we need to discuss about that, but first, consider something else interesting about how Paul taught humility. Eve-Marie Becker, a New Testament scholar who studied humility in Pauline theology, observed that in Philippians 2:3, "Paul coins a term that is not attested in Greek literature prior to him."[6] He did this to reframe and redefine the word in a brand-new context—which would be especially needed in Philippi, where the Greco-Roman culture was well established.[7] (The irony is, as Paul was writing this countercultural letter to the church in Philippi, he was most likely sitting in Roman imprisonment!)

Paul invented a new term to shake up people's view of humility, to drop all the negativity around it, and to lead them into a new mindset. He was bringing the kingdom of God into his culture. While his culture's concept of humility was based on an anthropocentric (human-centered) view, Paul's concept of it was based on a theocentric (God-centered) view. It was informed by the Scriptures, in which he was well-versed.

Throughout the Old Testament, the God-centered concept of humility is *positive*. This would have been shocking for the Greco-Roman world (New Testament time period)—just as it is for us now, in our culture. The running theme throughout the Old Testament is a gracious God lovingly choosing the lowly and weak, saving them, and lifting them up.

Deuteronomy 7:7 tells us that God "had his heart set" on his people, and it wasn't because they were strong and mighty and massive in number. They were the opposite—weak, feeble, and small in number. Unimpressive as they were, he chose them and covered them with his life-changing, covenantal love. We read, "Because the LORD loved you and kept the oath he swore to your ancestors, he brought you out with a strong hand and redeemed you from the place of slavery, from the power of Pharaoh king of Egypt" (Deuteronomy 7:8).

In 1 Samuel 2 we see that God didn't leave the "poor" in their despair. Verse 7 speaks of how the Lord "humbles" and "exalts." Verse 8 says, "He raises the poor from the dust and lifts the needy from the trash heap. He seats them with noblemen and gives them a throne of honor. For the foundations of the earth are the LORD's; he has set the world on them."

This has been the heart of our God all along. When we are low, he lifts us up. The exalted, mighty one reaches down to us to unite us with him.

He did it as Yahweh with the Israelites.

He did it as the Father sending the Son and as the Son becoming human.

He did it as Jesus with the sick and the sinful.

And he does it now, today, with you and me.

INVITING STABILITY AND COMMUNITY

Our modern situation, in some ways, is not terribly different from Paul's. It's kind of wild—even with technological advancements and cultural developments, some things seem to stay the same. The powerful, strong, and rich are the ones who win. The poor, weak, and lowly are the ones who lose. So people assume, *If you don't want to lose, don't be associated with losers. If you want to win, do whatever it takes to gain more human control, strength, and power.*

Paul redefined humility as something to be desired, not despised, and so can we.

When we see humility from a God-first perspective, it will place us in the safe, secure, and strong hands of the Creator of the universe. However, if we view humility through a human-first perspective, it will lead us to rely on our own feeble and fragile strength.

WHEN WE SEE HUMILITY FROM A GOD-FIRST PERSPECTIVE, IT WILL PLACE US IN THE SAFE, SECURE, AND STRONG HANDS OF THE CREATOR OF THE UNIVERSE.

One final thing is important for us to know about the way Paul framed the H-word. He wrote to churches that were connected to each other in community. So humility for Paul was always multidirectional. The humble life involves total awareness of God, which allows us to be safely in community with the people of God.

This contrasts the monastic approach to life, which likely started well after Paul's era, around AD 251–356. Monks focused on separation from the world to foster their full devotion to God.[8] Their understanding of humility led them to turn away from the world and society.[9] Notice how different this was from what we see in Paul's teaching. He had presented humility as the secret to living as faithful citizens of the kingdom of God, as the "clothing" for the church to wear daily while they resided for a time in the city of humanity. The humble life is most abundant when it is lived out among the family of God.

We may be tempted to live a "private" humility, where we keep it hidden from the world. But as we've learned, humility was a way of life for Paul and the first-century church. It was disruptive, changing the social dynamics of a society built on power and privilege, and became the identity marker of the family of God. None of this could have happened if humility had been a private practice hidden from the world.

Today, you and I have an opportunity to create the same type of disruption in our spheres of influence.

Steve Jobs, the iconic founder and visionary of Apple, had what his coworkers referred to as a "reality distortion field." He was full of charisma and able to get his coworkers to see his vision and make it their own.[10]

I think we have the opportunity to live with a humility version of this—except it wouldn't be a distortion, because humility connects us with reality. Maybe it'd be a "humility reorientation field."

> THE HUMBLE LIFE INVOLVES TOTAL AWARENESS OF GOD, WHICH ALLOWS US TO BE SAFELY IN COMMUNITY WITH THE PEOPLE OF GOD.

We can act in selfless, not selfish, ways. We can reject societal classes that prevent us from hanging out with people who are in different tax brackets or cultural groups. We can make the fundamental commitment to treat every human being with dignity and worth because they were created in the image of God.

Let's imagine how this could look closer down to the ground:

- We can refuse to cut corners in our workplace, even though others are doing it and say it's "no big deal."
- We can excuse ourselves from conversations with friends when the topic shifts to gossip about someone else, even though it could be said it's just a discussion based on concern.
- We can speak up and speak out when we see others being belittled, even though it would be safer to keep quiet and mind our own business.
- We can share boldly and confidently with our neighbors and friends about how Jesus has brought us confidence in our souls and peace in our homes because we've trusted his good for us over our own vision of good.

Each time we do things like this, we create and make visible the humility reorientation field. We exude the peace that humility has established for us, which is a striking contrast to the chaos in people's lives.

We can give the people around us a vision of a future that is livable and accessible to them now because of the power and confidence humility brings.

CHAPTER 12

SAFEGUARD YOURSELF WITH IT (BUILD RESILIENCE)

SOME PEOPLE HAVE a soft spot in their hearts for puppies. I have a spot soft in my heart for sneakers. To be more precise, Jordans. Any kind.

I never had a legitimate pair of Jordans as a kid. My parents were very frugal, especially when it came to clothing and shoes. We had a yearly rhythm: a couple of weeks before the school year, my mom would load my younger siblings and me into our minivan and drive us *past* the Nike, Adidas, and Reebok stores until we arrived at the holy grail of family shoe stores: Payless.

My mom was always so excited to walk in that store. In fact, every parent I saw there looked happy. Every child, on the other hand, wore a sober expression.

"Oh, how nice!" my mom would gush. "They have a 'Buy One Get One 50 Percent Off' sale!"

Years later, as an adult, I would realize that this "special sale" was one that ran year-round, year after year.

I would go up and down the aisles looking for sneakers that looked almost like legit Jordans, even though I knew they'd never pass for the real thing. I'd grab the sad, not-really-like-Jordans shoes, then snag a backup pair (for 50 percent off!), because we all knew these things would fall apart in a couple of months.

On the first day of school, I would pray no one would pay attention to my knockoff shoes. I just wanted to make it through the day under the radar. But that was never how things worked for me.

My friends would be showing off their new Jordan 1s, or Jordan 11s, or the really cool Reebok pump shoes that promised you'd jump higher if you'd pump them up before you played basketball. My friends would take one look at my shoes and start mocking them. It was pretty humiliating. Every morning I put on those Payless shoes, it felt like I was heading into another day of humiliation.

Now, imagine: What if my Jordans dreams had come true and I'd had the right shoes to impress everyone? That would have felt awesome. I mean, that would have changed my life! I absolutely would've taken a ton of pride in that.

I have no doubt, though, that I eventually would've relied on that positive attention for my self-worth. I ultimately would've been chained to the pursuit of becoming whatever would prompt all that feel-good acceptance. My heart would be prone to the praise of my friends as they hyped me up because of those fresh Js. But here's the problem: I would've needed more and more things to continue fitting in and staying in favor, to keep up with the comparison game. The Jordans never would have been enough. Next, it would have been the name-brand hoodies, jeans, and socks. Yes, even the socks! Y'all, it's a race that has no end in sight, because it is a pursuit of praise that will never be enough.

My self-perception and sense of security would've been completely wrapped up in all that.

So let's play that out. Could I always be the coolest person in the room, forever? No. Somewhere along the line, I would be around people who had better stuff in their life—a degree, a job, a house, connections—and people who valued things I didn't have.

I'd eventually feel crushed, less than, inadequate. Humiliated. And my lack of humility would have put me there.

PROTECTING YOURSELF FROM HUMILIATION

Humility can actually prevent us from experiencing humiliation. It steers us away from counting on things that will only let us down. It keeps us from giving power to things that we shouldn't.

Can humility prevent *all* humiliation? I wish that were the case, but no. We can't control other people or what happens to us, and we can't escape our own human fallibility.

We can, however, control where we find our security, the tools we bring into every situation, and the way we respond to hard moments. We can allow humility to protect our hearts in the midst of the inevitable humiliations of life. We can let God equip us to face them and get through them. And as we do, we'll become stronger and better for it.

Earlier this year I started doing something that may feel totally ridiculous to you. That's okay; it felt ridiculous to me too. My friend Levi Lusko had been doing this thing called a "cold plunge," and he suggested I do it too. My immediate thought was, *That's crazy. No way am I doing that.* But I couldn't dispute the research that said it could help with anxiety, reduce inflammation, boost metabolism, and speed up muscle recovery from workouts.[1]

> WE CAN ALLOW HUMILITY TO PROTECT OUR HEARTS IN THE MIDST OF THE INEVITABLE HUMILIATIONS OF LIFE.

The thing is, that water is *so cold*.

I decided to try it but learn strategies for easing into it. One way was to start with water straight from a hose and plunge for two minutes. After you do that a few days, you add some ice to the hose water and plunge for three minutes. Then you build up to adding more ice and staying in the water for more than four minutes. Over time, your body acclimates to the cold water and you build resiliency, both physically and psychologically.

Now, what if, while you were in the cold plunge, even colder water was poured on you? You would feel the difference, definitely. It may startle you. But it wouldn't catch you off guard, and you would be able to endure it.

Humility is kind of like the cold plunge, and humiliation is like the colder-water pour. Humility equips us for handling difficulties. Humiliation creates panic and makes us question who we are. Humility keeps us aware of who we are in light of who God is and builds our sense of stability. Then, when things go sideways—we feel let down or put down or belittled—we are secure and grounded enough to weather it.

Like the cold plunge, humility is uncomfortable yet doable. It may have a cost, but that cost is so worth it when something worse comes along, threatening to derail us. We're better able to handle the colder-water pour because we've been doing the cold plunge. Humility builds our resilience so we can persevere through the inevitable humiliating moments of life.

> IF WE LACK HUMILITY, WE ARE IN A POSITION OF UNGUARDED VULNERABILITY TO HUMILIATION.

If we lack humility, we are in a position of unguarded vulnerability to humiliation. Like my story about the shoes, if I'd gotten the Jordans but I still had no humility, I would have become a prisoner to "the next best thing." And with my self-worth tied up in being seen as cool, I'd continually be only one mocking moment away from feeling crushed.

The same thing plays out in our lives when we put our confidence in achievements, relationships, or possessions, which promise security—but their promise is contingent on us perpetually having the next best thing. It requires relentless effort to stay at the top. At some point we'll realize these things truly don't provide security, and we'll be in a vulnerable place, where humiliation is waiting around the corner to undo us. Where humiliation is present, peace is short-lived.

Maybe for you, it's getting pulled into the comparison trap, or seeking people's praise, or avoiding any kind of criticism like the plague. One way or another, we all sometimes get caught up in how the world views us. And whenever we do, we've placed our worth in something that will always ultimately fail us.

Here is the good news. It doesn't have to be this way!

HOW ARE WE DEALING WITH FEAR?

All of these issues connect back to our fears and how we handle them. Let's not forget that fear is a natural human response to a perceived threat, as our physiology proves. When we face something like a snake, a part of our brain called the amygdala triggers a neurochemical response to deal with that fear.[2] God wired this response into humanity for the purpose of protection. So let's not feel shame about simply experiencing fear.

We all have a multitude of fears. I once discussed with some trusted friends what our fears were, and what surfaced was similar to the fears I mentioned in the introduction:

- afraid of not being good enough
- afraid of being a bad Christian

- afraid of not living up to expectations
- afraid of being hurt
- afraid of what the future looks like
- afraid of failure
- afraid of not being loved or needed
- afraid of screwing up my kids
- afraid of kids or family getting hurt
- afraid of being worthless
- afraid of financial instability
- afraid of being viewed as incapable
- afraid of wasting my life
- afraid of rejection

The *APA Dictionary of Psychology* defines *fear* as an intense emotion "aroused by the detection of imminent threat, involving an immediate alarm reaction."[3] We believe something bad will happen, and often, if that bad thing happens, the result is pain.

I would say that each of our fears has an accomplice. I call this the "fear + _____" concept. The blank refers to some type of humiliation that our fear is tied to. If we have a fear that never comes true, we feel humiliated that we were afraid in the first place. If we have a fear that does come true and we experience pain as a result, we are humiliated by that.

All of this, of course, produces an immense amount of stress, and you know what chronic stress does to us? It "contributes to high blood pressure, promotes the formation of artery-clogging deposits, and causes brain changes that may contribute to anxiety, depression, and addiction."[4]

Notice how fear is intimately connected to all of this and how prolonged stress makes us more prone to experience humiliation. This is why we really need to deal with our fears—by facing them and walking through them in a way God has designed.

Now, before you jump ship and try to avoid all of this, hang on. What I just said really is true: *God has a way for us to deal with our fear.* And if we can see what humility can give us in the midst of fear and humiliation, we don't have to be afraid

> GOD HAS A WAY FOR US TO DEAL WITH OUR FEAR.

of what humiliating moments will strip or take away from us.

I call this "the humility or humiliation equation." Here's what it looks like for me.

THE HUMILITY OR HUMILIATION EQUATION

I have a deep fear that I'm going to be found out as not actually smart. I have a recurring nightmare that someone is going to ask me what John 3:16 means and I'm going to panic and freeze. I'll forget the verse and won't have any response. Then people will find out I'm truly not that smart and therefore don't really have much worth.

So the *humiliation* equation for me is:

I fear people will realize I'm not smart, and when they do they will abandon me, and this will cause me pain.

I deal with my fear by trying to gain more control, strength, and power. I get more degrees. I control all the questions I'm asked so I'm never caught off guard. *If I can do this, I can prevent fear and avoid hurt*, I think.

The problem is, the ultimate result is that my fear is still there, and there will come a day when I won't have the answer, or I will let someone down. People will abandon me, or I will feel like a failure.

This will leave me humiliated.

The *humility* equation for me looks like this:

I fear people will realize I'm not smart, and when they do they will abandon me, and this will cause me pain.

Instead of trying to gain my own control, strength, and power, I turn to God and trust in his control, strength, and power.

I accept that it's impossible for me to know everything. I remind myself that my worth is not in what I do but in my status as a child of God. Because I am grounded in humility, I can rest safe and secure in my relationship with Jesus—even when I'm wrong, I don't know something, or I let someone down.

I face the fear because I'm confident that Jesus is with me, and I walk through the pain with the presence of Jesus by my side through the power of the Holy Spirit.

This is living out humility.

These humiliation and humility equations help me see my options of how I can respond to my fears and pain. It might help you too. Below is a simple exercise for you to consider. You can fill in the blanks and walk through what your equation would look like.

YOUR HUMILIATION EQUATION

I fear that _____, which will cause _____ (some kind of pain).

If I _____ (try to conjure my own control, strength, power), I can escape fear and avoid pain.

Ultimate result: My fear is still there, and my pain continues. My efforts don't solve my issues. I am humiliated.

YOUR HUMILITY EQUATION

I fear that _____, which will cause _____ (some kind of pain).

If I trust Jesus and _____ (humbly reach toward his power, strength, and control), I will be equipped to deal with my fear and pain.

Ultimate result: My fear is still there, and my pain continues. But humility helps me face my fear with faith in Jesus. It leads me to rely on the Spirit's power to process my pain and get to the other side of it. I am humbled.

Let's not expect a life without fear and pain, friends. While we cannot escape these things, we do get to choose how we handle them.

THE MOMENTS THAT SHAPE YOU

Let me tell you about a mistake I recently made that created an opportunity for humility to protect me from humiliation.

As I was working through edits on this book, my editor, Carrie, caught something in a small section of my Bible teaching that she was curious about since she'd read something different. She asked about it. I looked at that section of teaching and came to the realization that I was wrong.

That's right. I—the theologian, the one with the PhD—was wrong. I'd made a mistake.

I considered my options of response. How could I frame this in a way that didn't make me look totally dumb and call into question my value, worth, and qualifications? Then I realized it was simple.

I just needed to say, "I was wrong, and thank you for helping me and saving me from making a mistake." And that is the exact note I left for her.

Yeah, I dealt with impostor syndrome. I went into some negative thoughts about myself. But I also realized that this was a means of sanctification in my life.

I'm human.

I'm fallible.

I make mistakes.

I need others to help me and point out my errors.

I can either hide behind a shallow and fabricated facade of pride masquerading as confidence or I can embrace the gift of humility, which places me safe and secure in the capable hands of Jesus.

Was this uncomfortable for me? Yes. Was it worth it? A resounding yes. Becoming aware that I was wrong led me into an acceptance of my weakness, and this will serve as a safeguard for me against future humiliation! Making mistakes will not ruin me. My self-worth won't be tied to an image of perfection. And this is so freeing because perfection is unattainable on this side of eternity! I can keep on accepting moments of weakness as opportunities to depend on God and to grow.

You're going to be staring down your own mistakes and weaknesses before long—it's the human way. Whenever you do, remember this: Weakness is not our enemy. It is the perfect ingredient in the soil of humility for Jesus to plant and cultivate his strength.

> WEAKNESS IS NOT OUR ENEMY. IT IS THE PERFECT INGREDIENT IN THE SOIL OF HUMILITY FOR JESUS TO PLANT AND CULTIVATE HIS STRENGTH.

Will it be uncomfortable for you? Yes. But will it be worth it? Absolutely.

Don't let the fact that it's hard and painful blind you from the big gain: these moments are sanctifying and good for our souls.

It's okay to be human. We make mistakes. What we do with those mistakes and how it shapes us into who we are becoming is of eternal value.

Friends, whenever you're dealing with insecurity, instability, or just the unknown, know that there is a way forward. There's a way to face your fears, weakness, and pain and stay rooted in humility.

CHECK IN WITH YOUR COUNSELOR

Now, as we've said, that way forward is not easy. In our moments of weakness, we need help—someone to meet us in our struggle and steer us toward the hard, right path.

We need a Counselor.

We need the Holy Spirit, who not only gives us the gift of humility but also empowers us to live a life of humility.

Sadly, conversations about the Holy Spirit today can be overly mystical or stripped of all mystery and power. But look how Jesus described the Holy Spirit in John 16: "It is for your benefit that I go away, because if I don't go away the Counselor will not come to you. If I go, I will send him to you. When he comes, he will convict the world about sin, righteousness, and judgment" (vv. 7–8).

I love the language of "counselor"—someone who provides important and specialized wisdom in the situations we need it the most. For some reason this always makes me think of old mafia movies where they have a "family counselor" who gives counsel on all things related to law, money, and strategy with the family business. "Not an exact correlation here, Joel," you might reply. I won't argue that. The Holy Spirit is our perfect Counselor. Unlike those mafia movies, where the counsel always seems to involve *breaking the law*, the Spirit of God leads us in *living according to his law*.

Jesus said the Spirit would convict the world about sin and lead his followers into truth (John 16:13). In other words, the Holy Spirit is what we desperately need in order to live out humble obedience in the way of Jesus. He is there to inform and guide us on a daily basis.

Every morning when I'm about to get dressed, I open my phone to two important apps that help me make the most important decision of my day: what shoes I will wear. (I meant it when I said this is my thing.)

The Calendar app tells me if I'll be sitting most of the day (foam cushion sneakers, please) or standing a lot (regular sneaker soles, sure). The Weather app tells me if it will be rainy (water resistant material it is) or sunny (anything goes!).

We need the spiritual equivalent of these apps to help us make wise decisions that will protect us from humiliation. And then we need to be responsive.

We've got to put off the "old self" and put on the "new self," Colossians 3:9–10 tells us, because we are being renewed as we become like Jesus.

A couple of verses later we read, "As God's chosen people, holy and dearly loved, *clothe yourselves* with compassion, kindness, *humility*, gentleness and patience" (v. 12 NIV).

And putting on the "new self" and our humility clothes reflects what we read in Romans 13:14: "Put on the Lord Jesus Christ, and make no provision for the flesh to gratify its desires."

KEEP CHOOSING HUMILITY IN YOUR HEART. KEEP CHOOSING THE WAY OF JESUS, HIS MINDSET, ATTITUDE, AND CHARACTERISTICS.

What do all these verses point to? Keep choosing humility in your heart. Keep choosing the way of Jesus, his mindset, attitude, and characteristics.

We can do this only in partnership with the Holy Spirit. We turn to him, and he gives us the discernment, conviction, and power we need.

It is something we are meant to do continually, the way clothing ourselves is a daily ritual and rhythm of life. It is not a one-and-done act.

It is also something we must be intentional about doing, just as we make the intentional decision to put on clothes every day. In fact, the goal is to be intentional about doing it *throughout* the day too.

Imagine if you made the right clothing decisions in the morning based on sunny predictions, but then at midday, rumbling, dark clouds show up out of nowhere. What do you do? If you're like me, you get drenched in the rain and it is what it is. Or, if you are like my wife, you pull out the "worst-case scenario" jacket you have on hand to protect you. You adjust. And you reach for your source of help.

"Midday adjustments" are meant to be part of the daily practice of humility. Yes, spend time in the morning preparing your heart in God's Word. (In fact, at the end of this book, there is a Getting Grounded in Scriptural Humility section you can use for your personal devotions.) But also take some touch-base moments with the Spirit throughout the day.

Maybe it's during your evening commute, when you think about a mistake you made at work. Or on a coffee break when memories of feeling put down by a friend come to mind. Or at lunch when you remember a moment of not measuring up to someone else.

Perhaps no emotional sting comes to mind, but you still take a minute to assess where you are today with depending on the Spirit and where you want to be tomorrow.

And you talk with God about all of it. This conversation is so important. I usually find myself having this conversation during a workout or while I'm walking to the bus stop to wait for my kids to get home. Sometimes it's a long conversation, but most of the time it's a quick chat. This is what it sounds like for me.

God, I really need you to tell me who I am and what I'm worth.

I know my value doesn't come from performance or from positive attention from others because this is what you've said and repeated in your Word. Help me believe it and trust it.

I know you love me when I'm weak, when I get things wrong, when I feel hurt.

I know I am safe with you. I can become stronger with you. Thank you and help me not to forget this.

God, how do you want me to lean into you more? Show me.

How do you want to grow me? Shape me.

Keep me in step with you. Lead me.

Every moment you accept truth from the Holy Spirit and align with him, more humility and strength is deposited into your soul. Over time, it changes you.

> EVERY MOMENT YOU ACCEPT TRUTH FROM THE HOLY SPIRIT AND ALIGN WITH HIM, MORE HUMILITY AND STRENGTH IS DEPOSITED INTO YOUR SOUL.

Imagine a future you walking into every room—at work, with family, in social settings—with a humble confidence formed by the Holy Spirit. How powerful and stabilizing would it feel to be certain that, regardless of any situation you walk into (positive or negative), you are connected to him, his love, and his resources?

Whatever would happen, you'd know in your bones: *God's got me. I'm going to be okay. He will get me through it.*

PART 4

LIVING THE SECURE, PEACEFUL LIFE

CHAPTER 13

IT'S MEANT TO BE MUTUAL

WE ARE A dog family through and through. As long as Britt and I have been married, we've had at least one dog, usually two.

Our first dog was a Lab-shepherd mix named Leonidas (named after the famous Spartan king) who should have been named Houdini, because he never met a crate he couldn't get out of.

Then came a Lab-beagle mix named Bella (yep, *Twilight*) who has been with us for more than thirteen years now. She was there to welcome our firstborn, Liam, when we first brought him home from the hospital and literally saved his life once by keeping him from falling down the stairs.

We now also have Lady (I'll let you guess the movie/book), who is 100 percent German shepherd and sheds worse than we could have ever imagined.

Our kids love dogs too, and it has been a very special thing to watch them grow alongside our family dogs.

Being a dog family means we've learned a lot about how to train dogs. One of our favorite family TV shows to watch has been

Dog Whisperer with Cesar Millan. Cesar's ability to rehabilitate dogs and train people is spectacular. One thing I've always found interesting about his approach is how he corrects dogs when they do something they aren't supposed to do. He gives them a touch on the neck or, in more serious cases, forces them to lie on their side in a submissive manner and to wait for his permission to get back up. He'd explain dog psychology to viewers, saying dogs needed these types of messages to help them understand their place in the pack (or their dog family).

People have different opinions on this, but I can tell you firsthand that this is exactly what I saw take place with wild dogs during a visit to India. They were all over the area I was in, and one day I saw a dog lying down in submission with another dog standing over it. I pointed it out to my friend, who lived in India. He simply said, "That's how they know who the boss is."

Now, what may be acceptable for animals is, of course, totally unacceptable for humans. Why? Because humans are made in the likeness and image of God. We studied this earlier; we know how special it is to be made in God's image and the responsibility we have toward one another because of that. Can you imagine if, in our everyday lives, we saw humans forcing other humans to submit the way animals do? Surely (hopefully) even our basic moral compass would prompt us to put a stop to such ugly behavior.

Yet I think people in our society actually do experience a type of forced submission and silencing. It happens in a variety of ways—emotional, spiritual, psychological, even physical. Maybe it's happening to you. You may have some concern at work and the response is simply "Get over it." Or there is tension or conflict with a friend, and instead of dealing with it, you are being gaslighted into believing it's not even an issue. Earlier we talked about how this can fuel our hesitation about humility. We've seen people weaponize it, using it to control others, so it feels really unsafe.

So, naturally, we reach for safety and find ourselves thinking, *Humility is great as long as it's expected of* others *and not required of* me. It's a self-preservation instinct.

But isn't that the same attitude of a person who's forcing someone else to submit to them?

Well, ouch.

I know. This is hard.

But hang with me. There is a way for us to be safe and secure in our relationships. There is a way to enjoy the presence of other people without the threat of being taken advantage of. And, if we do experience hurt (because we can't control others), we can still safeguard our hearts to endure the hurt and be stronger on the other side.

All of this is dependent on our perspective in relationships.

THE TWO-WAY ROAD OF BIBLICAL HUMANITY

We're going to look at two perspectives in relationships, and the first one is about power and control. Someone feels threatened by someone or something, and they react by becoming threatening to others. It makes humility a monologue when it's meant to be a dialogue.

Humility as a monologue is spoken *at* others, meaning someone forces someone else into a type of humility (not a biblical one). They weaponize it to manipulate others. It is tied to foundational fears they have and how they've tried to deal with them by gaining control, strength, and power (as we discussed in part 2).

When humility is weaponized, it turns into a vicious tool that results in humiliation. And, of course, everyone is desperately trying to avoid humiliation: in our jobs, in our relationships, in any public situation. It's been this way throughout our lives, starting when we were kids.

For me as a kid, as one of the few Indians in a neighborhood with racism issues, I always felt like humiliation could be right around the corner. I didn't belong in any group—Black, white, Latino, Asian. (Yes, even Asians. Apparently, Indians didn't belong to the subcontinent of Asia. We couldn't be Indian *and* Asian!) I was constantly anticipating the next moment I'd have to endure humiliation over my skin color. Over my background. Over the type of food I ate. (I refused to bring homemade lunches to school because it would be rice and curry, and I was terrified of being made fun of.)

The one place I felt safe was on the basketball court. Sure, I was a short Indian kid, but I had good handles and a behind-the-back crossover move I'd perfected. I can still hear the *oohs* and *aahs* when I would cross over a super aggressive defender at midcourt. I could hear the whispers: "Yo, the Indian kid can ball." The basketball court was my safe space.

But that changed one day when I did a nice crossover and followed up with a layup, and someone yelled, "Yo, the Hindu crossed you over!"

I looked around, wondering who this Hindu was. Then I realized everyone was looking at me.

"I'm not Hindu. I'm actually Christian," I quickly tried to explain, but no one heard me over the yells about the Hindu. In a split second I went from being *Joel* to *Hindu* in the eyes of those kids.

This hurt deeply for a few reasons. First, while Hinduism is a major religion in India, not all Indians are Hindu. Second, I was Christian, and calling me Hindu felt deeply disrespectful. Third, I was scared to speak up for myself because I was afraid of what people would think of me. It hurt to feel pushed into a corner like that.

So I just let it slide, feeling like I couldn't do anything about it. Eventually I took that offensive term and flipped it around and wore it like a badge of honor. For the rest of my elementary school years, my nickname continued to be Hindu.

When I look back at that experience, I realize those kids nicknamed me Hindu because it was a way for them to humble and humiliate me. It put me in their sphere of power and influence. It took away my personal agency and forced me into a posture of humility, into a humiliation that would stop me from speaking out. The other kids' laughter and instant acceptance of the nickname only reinforced all of this to me.

After having this kind of humbling, humiliating experience, why would I, of all people, call us to reclaim the lost virtue of humility?

Because any type of humility we experience that results in our humiliation is not biblical humility. One of our sinister Enemy's ancient tactics is to take biblical virtues and turn them into soul-crushing vices. So we have to remember that pursuing true humility does not mean pursuing humiliation.

The kind of humility God leads people into is not a monologue—a one-directional conversation that leaves room for one-sided humiliation. It's a dialogue—a conversation between two people with expectations on both sides. There is a cost to both parties and a requirement that both parties listen *and* speak. One person speaks while the other listens, then they switch roles.

How does the person listening know when it is time to start talking? Through attentive listening and confident engagement.

How does the person speaking know it's time to hear from the other person? Through willing submission and a desire to hear from the other person.

If the listener doesn't exercise confidence to respond, the discussion will always be a monologue. You get the same result if the speaker does not willingly submit to hearing: the conversation will remain a monologue. It's only when *both parties exercise mutual sub-mission to each other* that a monologue turns into a dialogue. And that, my friend, is the secret to healthy humility in our relation-ships. Mutual submission.

You may be thinking, *Things have gone from bad to worse. Not only do we have to embrace humility; now we have to deal with submission!*

No. And yes.

No, because I'm not talking about the kind of submission that keeps people down or silences them, the kind that protects the strong and hurts the weak. That is not at all where we are going.

And yes, because we are indeed going to talk about submission within human relationships. I get that it's uncomfortable for many of us. But don't give up on me now. There's something for us here. God can work powerfully in and through hearts that are sincerely submitted to him and to each other.

A FAMILY LOVE LIKE NO OTHER

We're going to look closely at Scripture to discover this, but before we do, I want to touch on something really quick here at the jump. The passage we're starting with is from a letter the apostle Paul wrote to the church in Thessalonica, a community that was already united together in Christ. So this message is meant for Jesus fol-lowers. It's intended to guide people who profess to be Christians in developing healthy humility in their relationships. Our next chap-ter will cover healthy and humble boundaries, which applies to all our relationships, with both Christians and non-Christians. But in this discussion, based on this part of Scripture, the context is relationships among believers.

The apostle Paul wrote,

About brotherly love: You don't need me to write you because you yourselves are taught by God to love one another. In fact, you are doing this toward all the brothers and sisters in the entire region of Macedonia. But we encourage you, brothers and sisters, to do this even more, to seek to lead a quiet life, to mind your own business, and to work with your own hands, as we commanded you, so that you may behave properly in the presence of outsiders and not be dependent on anyone. (1 Thessalonians 4:9–12)

Paul started by affirming something the church was already doing: showing their love for one another just as God had taught them. In fact, their love was so contagious and visible that the entire region of Macedonia had been impacted.

Thessalonica was a diverse city ethnically and socially. People were typically grouped by their ethnic background or economic situation, which then dictated their social status. It would have cost the people in this church to profess saving faith in Jesus—both personally and publicly. Their conversion might have broken a family relationship or cut their ties with a societal group they depended on for their livelihood.

In this passage, Paul introduced a new family relationship—one not of genetic or ethnic commonality but of spiritual commonality.

We have to wonder, *How?* How did people who had nothing in common, who were once at odds with one another, become "brothers and sisters" who loved each other?

They were united in the work of Jesus, who hung on a cross, defeating death through death. Jesus turned enemies who were at war with each other into members of one family who would die for one another!

This new family dynamic came with a responsibility: to love one another as brothers and sisters.

Paul referred to this group of believers as "brothers" or "sisters" at least nineteen times in this letter. When he talked about the love in their community, he used the Greek word that is a familial type of love. It is interesting to note that this word was used in the Greek world primarily to describe blood relationships among family members.[2] Why would Paul use this word here?

Let's look again at the context. Paul said they had been taught to love one another by God.

The love God had for humanity was expressed by sending his Son to the cross. In turn, this kind of love became the model of love for the church (John 3:16; Romans 5:8; Ephesians 5:1–2). Jesus also commanded his disciples to love one another just as he loved them (John 13:34–35, 15:12), and his love was executed in perfection on the cross.

It was there that Jesus spilled his divine blood in order to bring people who were once enemies into a new family.

It's completely wild, isn't it? *Enemies joined together by blood.* This is the power of Jesus! It's something only his divine blood can do.

So this is how the loving relationship starts, how the unity is established. Then the love is meant to continue through the process of reciprocity.

The phrase "one another" in 1 Thessalonians 4:9 comes from a Greek reciprocal pronoun (*allēlous*), and it is one of Paul's favorite phrases to describe the type of relationship believers should have with each other. It suggests two dimensions of communal identity that shape the life of Christians.

First, it suggests that believers care for one another without regard for social, economic, or ethnic position.

Second, the term indicates the equal status of all members within the group. There is no place for hierarchy in the family of God because all have been adopted into the family through the sacrifice of Jesus the Messiah. We all sit equally in the likeness and image of God under the authority and kingship of Jesus.

This is a posture of humility.

We recognize our entry into the family has nothing to do with what we have done but everything to do with what Jesus accomplished. This humble awareness leads us to pursue relationships of reciprocity with others. We invite others into our stories, which creates a pathway for an invitation into their stories.

We open ourselves up to the true unifying love between siblings that God can pour into us. We genuinely care about one another. We care about others' hurt because, in the family of God, their hurt is our hurt. We agonize over their plight because we feel it deeply, as we've been invited into that story.

Reciprocity is about matching each other. With the ferocity I show my love to you, you respond with the same ferocity back to me.

Is there a possibility someone won't respond with the same kind of love? Yes. That's the scary part. That's when the reciprocity is broken. It's why the *mutual* aspect of relationships is so vital.

> HUMILITY IS A CENTRAL COMPONENT OF ESTABLISHING AND KEEPING *ONE-ANOTHER* RELATIONSHIPS.

It's also why humility is a central component of establishing and keeping *one-another* relationships. Humility prompts us to give that love, and humility compels us to respond to that love.

RECIPROCITY IN ACTION

A few months after Ahmaud Arbery, Breonna Taylor, and George Floyd died and multiple other tragedies occurred around the world in 2020, communities were left reeling in confusion, grief, and anxiety. Questions of racial injustice and how Christians should respond were on the minds of pastors and Christians across the nation.

I get to attend a church where ethnicity and justice issues are discussed regularly, and I am so grateful for that. I go to Transformation Church in Fort Mill, South Carolina, where Derwin Gray (who wrote an incredible book called *How to Heal our Racial Divide*) serves as pastor and I serve on the teaching team. The small group I was a part of in 2020 included a Black family, a blended Black and white family, a blended Black and Latino family, and my own blended Indian and white family. After all those horrors in 2020, we met at our house and just sat together, stunned and devastated and trying to figure out how we should feel and respond to everything that was happening in our world.

One of the dads who is Black started talking about having the "talk" with his sons.

Halfway through the story a white dad interrupted him. "Wait, when you say 'the talk,' you're talking about sex, right?"

And then the discussion really began.

We all began to explain that "the talk" for many minority families had to do with what should and should not be done if we ever got pulled over by the police.

Different people shared their experiences. I shared how, since my kids are all different shades of brown, I had to have different conversations with them about how to handle getting pulled over.

I won't ever forget the tears in the eyes of the white dad at the end of the conversation. He said, "I need to have 'the talk' with my kids."

We all were kind of surprised and asked him why.

"Because our kids love each other. They are one family. I need to make sure my kids know how to act and respond if they are in the car and one of your kids is driving."

Every parent of color in my living room started sobbing. And within a few minutes, everyone in the living room, regardless of ethnicity or culture, was in tears.

This was the beauty of healthy humility in relationships rooted in mutual submission. This was reciprocity in action.

What happened over the course of forty-five minutes in my living room was an exchange of invitations and responses. Each person invited the others into their story. Each one responded in warm acceptance and care. And all of it was made possible through the unexpected but essential power of humility.

You may be wondering how this type of experience could be possible for you.

Well, someone always has to go first. This is the scariest part of being in a relationship that is reciprocal. Maybe the next step for you is to make the decision to be the one who takes initiative.

Just think: Everyone in that small group started out as strangers. Then they progressed to acquaintances. Then friends. Then reciprocal family members. Every step of the way involved one person offering connection and another responding in kind. And, of course, that's how the entire progression began.

Where can you go first? How can you show reciprocity in your friendships through the power of humility? Is it a coffee with a friend you've been wanting to invest in? Is it a walk with a neighbor? Is it a dinner with that family from church you've told, "Someday we'll get together!" One of the greatest gifts you can give yourself and others is simply going first.

So let's not wait.

Take out your phone and open your Notes app. Jot down the first three names that pop into your mind.

Now text them . . . you go first!

CHAPTER 14

A SOFT HEART CAN BE FIRM

I'M SURE YOU'VE been holding on to a bunch of what-ifs.

Maybe the idea of humility is starting to sound good and even like something worth pursuing. But what about all the challenges and drawbacks?

What if the people I'm around aren't Christians?
What if they say they're Christians but they definitely aren't acting like it?
What if people take advantage of me, viewing humility as weakness?
What if I get hurt and humiliated?
What if the humble life is unlivable because I'm in a constant state of fear that others will walk all over me?

All these what-ifs, along with others you've had, are totally valid. But I want to whisper some good news to your heart. You can be confident that there's a way to live a life of humility and

- not get walked over;
- not be paralyzed by fear;
- not allow humiliation to break you; and
- not be manipulated and controlled.

It requires something that has long been neglected by Christians because we've misunderstood it. In a way, it's a sibling to humility. It allows us to keep our hearts soft while remaining firm in our convictions and staying safe relationally, socially, and spiritually.

WE NEED BOUNDARIES ROOTED IN HUMILITY.

What we need are boundaries rooted in humility.

A GOD IDEA

A favorite part of my job is when our Proverbs 31 team meets at Lysa's house for a theology study day. On one of those days, I approached our study table to find everyone chatting, probably about Taylor Swift or some mystery crime podcast someone was listening to—two things that are completely uninteresting to me. But I acknowledge this is what I signed up for when I joined the staff of a women's ministry.

At this point our team had just finished working on Lysa's book *Forgiving What You Can't Forget*, and we knew it was only a matter of time until she had an idea for her next book. When the conversation died down, Lysa addressed all of us with, "I'm just wondering . . ." which is basically Lysa language for *I've become fascinated and can't stop thinking about the next thing that's going to come out of my mouth.*

She continued, "I think something we've all really struggled with—and something that adds so much chaos to our lives—is our lack of or inability to establish boundaries."

Then she looked at me and said, "Joel, I think boundaries are so important. I actually think they aren't just a good idea; they are a God idea. Do you agree?"

It took me a second to take in what I'd just heard and run it through the never-ending "Is this theologically accurate?" filter called my mind.

"Wow, that's a pretty big claim, Lysa," I replied. "Let's spend some time studying boundaries in the Bible and see where that takes us."

Long story short, over a thousand hours of research later, I could confidently say Lysa was absolutely correct. Throughout the research process I found that, while boundaries are God's idea, they can (like anything else) be misused. If we have unhealthy motivations, or if we implement them without caution, we can create more pain and frustration. When we handle boundaries the right way, though, they can bring us peace and make our relationships healthier. And that's true even if the cost of a healthy relationship is a pause, distance, or goodbye in the relationship (Romans 12:18).

So what's the secret to establishing healthy boundaries and having the courage and conviction to keep those boundaries in place? (I know you know the answer to this!) It's humility.

While I was studying boundaries in Scripture, I noticed how God established boundaries with humanity: *from a compassionate and kind heart*. God's heart posture toward his image bearers was always rooted in compassion, grace, and mercy—but that didn't mean boundaries weren't needed, or that he waffled and changed his mind about them. No, he confidently carried out the consequences of broken boundaries, all the while maintaining his loving, gracious character.

THE FIRST GOSPEL GOODBYE

The first place we see this in Scripture is what I refer to as "the First Gospel Goodbye."

In Genesis 1 and 2, God established his relationship with Adam and Eve within the context of a covenant. A basic definition of a covenant is a contract that has expectations from two parties. God established a covenant with Adam and Eve and provided safety, security, and stability for them in Eden under the single condition that they refrain from eating the fruit of "the tree of the knowledge of good and evil" (Genesis 2:17). This was the boundary.

As we discussed in chapter 7, Adam and Eve ended up eating that forbidden fruit, committing the first sin of humankind together. What did they deserve as a result of their sin? Death.

Yet God in his kindness and mercy intervened.

We might wonder, *Wait, did God threaten a consequence he never intended to keep? Did he flake on the consequence of death?*

Well, not exactly. In the moment Adam and Eve ate the fruit, they did experience a type of death—a spiritual death, as their beautiful union with God was ruptured. When sin entered the relationship between God and humanity, the intimacy between them was ruined. But, because his heart for humanity was still compassionate, God ensured that this ruin would not be eternal.

This is where things get so interesting.

It turns out that when God carried out the consequence for humans breaking his boundary for them, it was *good news*. This is where I get the phrase "the First Gospel Goodbye."

In both the Hebrew and Greek languages, the words translated as "to proclaim/herald good news" (*basar*; *euangelizomai*) have to do with the proclamation or delivery of good news, usually within a military context.[1] Let's remember that in the ancient world they had no FaceTime, WhatsApp, or sophisticated communication systems that could deliver important news worldwide in seconds. What the ancient world had were fast horses and people who could ride them. So when an army had a decisive victory, the king would assign his fastest horse and best rider to run to every other battlefield to announce the good news that the war had been won. The smaller battles and skirmishes going on everywhere else could stop! Sadly, for those places the horseman reached last, people kept on dying in battle until the good news of victory reached them. That's what the biblical word *gospel* is associated with—*life-or-death-stakes* good news.

And that's part of the root meaning of the phrase "the First Gospel Goodbye." It was in fact "good news" that God exiled Adam and Eve from Eden.

Joel, I need a little help here, you may be thinking. *How in the world is there good news here? This seems like news of defeat, not victory.*

First, you are a brilliant theologian for asking this important question. Why is the sending of Adam and Eve out of Eden good news? Because if they'd stayed in Eden, eating of the Tree of Life, they would have stayed in a perpetual state of separation from God. This would have been true defeat. But God in his kindness and compassion—and I would go a step further and suggest in humility[2]—acted on behalf of humanity for their greater good.

Now I want to give you some biblical evidence for why this is a "Gospel Goodbye." There's a lot to pull out even from one verse, Genesis 3:21. It says, "The LORD God made clothing from skins for the man and his wife, and he clothed them."

1. *Lives Lost for Their Benefit*

     Where did these skins come from? Living skins can come only from living creatures, which means innocent animals lost their lives to cover the shame and sin of Adam and Eve.

There is a gospel echo here. Laced into this tragic moment is the anticipation of how sin would be undone through the humble death of Jesus. The innocent Son of God gave his life to cover the shame and sin of all humanity.

2. *An Exchange of Better Clothing*

Adam and Eve first tried to cover up their shame with clothes made of leaves. They basically tried to exercise their own control, strength, and power to deal with their fear (being naked) and the hurt of broken relationships. A nice try, but how far would leaf clothes take them outside of Eden? Not a heck of a lot of protection there.

So God clothed Adam and Eve with something more suitable as they headed out into the world. He provided an exchange of clothes. (Sound familiar? Maybe an exchange of yokes?!)

3. *A Gesture of Inheritance*

The language of "clothing" for Adam and Eve is rooted in a rich Ancient Near Eastern tradition of kings presenting their children with clothing as a sign of inheritance rights.[3]

Even in the midst of a needed sacrifice, Adam and Eve experienced a sense of belonging and blessing. The reality of sorrow mingled with elements of goodness. This gift not only brought an immediate good (clothing) but also promised a future good (inheritance).

Yes, a boundary had been established and broken, and a consequence followed. But look at the way God handled the situation. It was full of grace, mercy, and compassion.

God sent Adam and Eve out of Eden for their ultimate good (and our ultimate good). The loving Creator gave his image bearers what they didn't deserve. This "First Gospel Goodbye" is a spectacular display of his grace-laced humility toward humanity.

But there is something even more important we can see in this example: how God maintained a soft and compassionate heart even as he remained firm about boundaries.

This is the power of humility when it intersects with boundaries.

ESTABLISHING HUMBLE BOUNDARIES

I wonder how you feel about boundaries. Does hearing the word make you squirm because you find them hard to stick to? Or maybe you've got the "sticking to them" part down, but you sense them creating a lot of emotional distance in your relationships. Or you could be thinking, *Okay, back up. How about you tell me what boundaries actually look like?*

Well, broadly speaking, you live with boundaries all the time, like when you drive the speed limit or keep your Venmo password private (no matter how much your kids beg for it). The traffic rules are in place for the ultimate safety of everyone. And you keep your kids out of your bank account so you can keep spending money on things like groceries and the mortgage, not truckloads of candy and Disney World trips.

There are various types of boundaries in relationships—physical, emotional, intellectual, financial.

Perhaps there's someone you have a harder time with one-on-one, so you prioritize associating with them in group settings.

Or there's someone who continually makes choices that baffle you, but you avoid making efforts to control them, accepting that it's not your responsibility.

Maybe there is a sensitive topic you decide not to bring up around some people. That's the case with my family. One particular issue is so personal and painful that we've put a boundary in place not to discuss it around those who are most sensitive to it. Why? Because we want to care for those sensitive family members. So we talk about our own pain related to that topic, continuing to process what we can in a healthy way, apart from them.

Boundaries are there for everyone's good. But many of us struggle with them because they always come with a cost, both to us and to others. We have to find ways to gracefully say no and to connect with others within a boundary. There are real consequences, as there should be. As Jim has said, "A boundary without a consequence is just a mere suggestion."[4] And this is the rub! We all want boundaries to keep us safe, but we also don't want to hurt others' feelings. We long for peace and stability that we feel deep in our souls, and sometimes we can't tell whether boundaries will truly foster this or just create more strife.

Honestly, they truly can create more strife . . . unless you have humility.

COMPASSIONATE, CONFIDENT, AND CONNECTED

Humility keeps our hearts soft and gives us the courage to do what we must to establish and maintain peace.

When we're humble, we know how God views *others*. So we treat other image bearers with kindness and dignity, showing respect for their God-given worth, even when we have boundaries in place. We pursue peace with others.

When we're humble, we also know how God views *us*. We're his cherished children, whom he loves with a sacrificial,

> HUMILITY KEEPS OUR HEARTS SOFT AND GIVES US THE COURAGE TO DO WHAT WE MUST TO ESTABLISH AND MAINTAIN PEACE.

never-ending love. So we won't devalue ourselves by continuing to put ourselves in unhealthy situations. He makes us confident in having boundaries for the sake of our well-being. We pursue peace in our inner lives and know it will eventually spread to our outer lives.

Now, what happens when we have boundaries *without* humility? We run the risk of having a concrete heart. We can lose the love and sense of connection we need to live in harmony with others.

A concrete heart thinks first and foremost about *what's best for me.* It seeks out *my own good* above anyone else's. When we have this type of hard heart, we'll definitely stick to our boundaries, but our relationships will begin to fracture. We will go from living in community to living in isolation. It is a tragedy, and it isn't what God has for us.

God wants us to live in community, to have soft and compassionate hearts, and to be unafraid to make difficult decisions about boundaries, because we know there is a greater good on the other side: peace internally and externally.

The Hebrew word for peace is *shalom*, and it has to do with both the absence of pain and the presence of peace. It is a return to being "whole and complete"[5] and, in a sense, a return to the vision of Eden prior to the fall.

> HUMILITY ALLOWS US TO LOVINGLY KEEP BOUNDARIES SO WE CAN AVOID CHAOS AND INVITE PEACE.

Saint Augustine said, "Where there is humility, there is peace."[6] I would build on this and say, "Where there are humble boundaries, there will be the possibility for enduring peace." Boundaries establish order, and order is necessary to experience peace. Where there is disorder, there will be chaos. This is true emotionally, physically, and spiritually. Humility allows us to lovingly keep boundaries so we can avoid chaos and invite peace.

Earlier I talked about a difficult family dynamic and how we established boundaries that had everyone in mind. The simple consideration of other people as we establish boundaries is an example of humility on display. Now, imagine that same scenario and one of us instead thought, *Well, I need to process my thoughts and feelings whenever I want to, regardless of what others are feeling. If I can't do that freely with whoever is around, I won't even come to the family gathering.*

> HUMILITY IS AN AWARENESS OF GOD THAT ALLOWS US TO KNOW OURSELVES AND HOW TO RELATE TO OTHERS.

This is an example of a boundary that lacks humility. Remember, humility is an awareness of God that allows us to know ourselves and how to relate to others. An approach to boundaries that places you as the only one who matters and disregards other people is evidence of pride. This approach will eventually cause relationships to fall apart.

THE HUMBLE RELATIONSHIP GUIDEBOOK

If we were to make a guidebook for the entire humble Christian life, Romans 12:10–18 would be a key part of it. The apostle Paul started the discussion in Romans 12:3 with a framework of humility, warning people not to think of themselves "more highly" than they should. "Be honest in your evaluation of yourselves," he told them (NLT).

What follows in verses 10 through 18 is wisdom we can use to keep our hearts soft as we maintain boundaries.

We are to love one another as siblings, honestly and without hypocrisy. And—I love this part—to "take the lead in honoring one another" (v. 10).

Verses 12 through 15 list actions to take:

- Rejoice in hope.
- Be patient in affliction.
- Persist in prayer.
- Share with the saints in all needs.
- Pursue hospitality.
- Bless those who persecute you.
- Bless, don't curse.
- Rejoice with those who rejoice.
- Weep with those who weep.

In verse 16, we find a collection of powerful pursuits, the secrets to accomplishing the list above. "Live in *harmony* with one another. Do not be *proud*; instead, associate with the *humble*. Do not be wise in your own estimation."

Something to know about biblical authors: sometimes they used sentence structures that held meaning, so the arrangement of ideas itself conveyed a message. One sentence built on another and ultimately hinged on a statement that brought definition to the surrounding text. The technical term for this is *chiasm*, and I think Paul was using this strategy in these verses.

It looks something like this.

Love one another deeply as brothers and sisters. Take the lead in honoring one another.

Do not lack diligence in zeal; be fervent in the Spirit; serve the Lord. Rejoice in hope; be patient in affliction; be persistent in prayer.

Share with the saints in their needs; pursue hospitality. Bless those who persecute you; bless and do not curse. Rejoice with those who rejoice; weep with those who weep.

Live in harmony with one another. Do not be proud; instead, associate with the humble. Do not be wise in your own estimation.

Do not repay anyone evil for evil. Give careful thought to do what is honorable in everyone's eyes.

If possible, as far as it depends on you, live at peace with everyone. Friends, do not avenge yourselves; instead, leave room for God's wrath, because it is written, Vengeance belongs to me; I will repay, says the Lord.

This means that if we want to make sense of how to live out the verses *around* verse 16—that is, verses 10–15 and 17–19—we need to look closely *here in verse 16.*

Living in harmony (or peace) with others requires us to abstain from pride (which leads to concrete hearts). It requires us to surround ourselves with people who are humble—people who don't think they are wise in their own estimation, who don't think of themselves first and others second, and who fight against the temptation of pride at every turn.

Humility, which we see throughout verse 16, is the hinge that makes the other verses actually livable. When you and I have a proper awareness of who we are in light of who God is, it changes everything.

We are intimately aware of the great mercy and kindness of God.

(So we can rejoice in hope. Be patient in affliction. Persist in prayer. And bless those who persecute us.)

We are more prone to show grace and mercy to other image bearers who are in the same position we are.

(So we can share with all the saints in all needs and pursue hospitality.)

We recognize that we're all fighting and struggling for godliness and holiness in a world that is trying to steer us off course, pushing us to give in to selfish ambition and pride.

(So we can rejoice and weep with others and live in harmony with them.)

Humility helps us identify what is hypocritical. When we truly know ourselves, it is more difficult to present a false version of ourselves or to entertain relationships with people who present fake versions of themselves.

(So we can let love be without hypocrisy.)

Now, how exactly can you apply all this Romans 12 wisdom to boundaries?

First, these verses can help you form a vision for when boundaries need to be established. The goal is harmony, so if there is disharmony, it is a sign that you may need to create a boundary or reevaluate your existing boundaries.

Next, these verses guide you in the right heart attitude to have while establishing and keeping boundaries. It's never about bitterness or resentment. It's about choosing healthy, wise ways to love and connect with each other.

Rest assured that if a relationship has brought you deep hurt, you can live out Romans 12 without becoming a doormat. You can keep your heart both protected and soft.

Perhaps the only way for you (and others) to experience peace is to pull back from daily communication with certain individuals. But whenever you do communicate with them, you remain kind and caring.

Or maybe you take a break from communication altogether for a while. As you do, you pray for that person—persistently. If it's too painful to pray for them, ask God to give you a heart that will be able to pray for them someday. This whole

> HUMILITY IS CRUCIAL FOR KEEPING A SOFT HEART WHENEVER WE MAKE HARD DECISIONS ABOUT BOUNDARIES.

thing is a process, and that's okay. But let's make a decision to be committed to the process, because it will bring about a personal good for us, which will help create an environment of peace.

Humility is crucial for keeping a soft heart whenever we make hard decisions about boundaries. This includes the times when peace is not possible with others.

"AS FAR AS IT DEPENDS ON YOU"

Romans 12:18 reads, "If possible, as far as it depends on you, live at peace with everyone."

It's important to note the construction of this sentence. It starts with a conditional clause: "if possible." This has huge implications for us in our relationships, especially when it comes to boundaries. Paul was saying that sometimes it's not possible to live at peace with someone.

How do we know if "living at peace" is possible? The next phrase helps answer that: "As far as it depends on you."

Now, if you and I were sitting at Starbucks and studying this passage, I would pause and ask you how you felt reading this. If you were honest with me, you might say, "That is *so unfair!* Why should I have to bear the responsibility of keeping the peace in a strenuous relationship? It's made up of two people—the status of peace shouldn't depend only on me!"

Friend, I feel you, I hear you, and, trust me, there is a part of me that agrees with you.

But I do want to flip the question and ask, What if Paul had written it another way? What if he'd said "as far as it depends *on them*"?

Now how are you feeling?

That would be even more devastating because it'd leave you

truly helpless. You'd be stuck as a bystander while someone else called all the shots.

So when verse 18 puts the ownership on you, it's actually a gift, not a burden. It's a gift because only you can know if you've done all that is possible. Only you have the power and ability to act on your own behalf and create a boundary. This verse is confirming your agency.

All right, let's say you have done everything within your power. What is your next priority?

Again, it's to live at peace with everyone. That's right! It's your goal in every scenario.

If it's possible to live at peace, you're shooting for living with peace.

And *if it's not possible* to live in peace—and you know because you've done everything you can to create peace in a relationship, and nothing has changed—the goal is still the same: to live at peace with all people.

Wait, though. How can that happen, since we just said "it's not possible"?

Well, you may have to establish boundaries, and those boundaries can create peace. Even if it means removing your presence from a relationship.

I know this is hard. And if we don't have humility as the soil of our souls to protect our hearts, it causes our hearts to become stone-cold. But humility keeps our hearts soft. While the relationship may not be restored, we can still cherish the peace that we have internally and externally.

Anything is possible in the kingdom of God and by the power of God. There is always hope for transformation, for a relationship to be restored in unexpected and inexplicable ways. But a key even to this is maintaining a humble heart that is receptive to this possibility.

Early on in my teenage years, I caused a lot of hurt for some people close to me. I acted out of selfishness, pride, arrogance, and a total disregard for others. As a result, those relationships became fractured and broken. I was the problem, I was the cause, and those people around me were the victims.

After a few years (and some needed maturing), I realized how destructive my behavior had been. I reached out to apologize to those people, acknowledging that the way I'd acted was unacceptable. For the majority of them, it was too little too late. The hurt had been too profound. While they did forgive me, the possibility of reconciliation was unlikely.

Fast-forward almost two decades later, and I ran into one of those old friends at an airport. We both had a layover and decided to grab some food together. We sat, we laughed, we caught up on life. In a surprising and unexpected way, God brought us back together. Since then we've slowly been building our relationship again. Two decades ago I never would have imagined this would be possible. And then I found myself in awe of how powerfully God had worked.

What did this require? Humility to own mistakes. Humility to accept boundaries that were placed on me (loss of relationship). Many of us may not have thought about how humility is necessary to be a recipient of boundaries. But we all will be on the giving or receiving end at some point, and humility is so valuable for us as we process through these situations. It also required the cultivation of humility as the soil of my Christian life to keep my heart soft and open to what God may do. I'm grateful and humbled that God worked the way he did. Restoration is never a guarantee, but when it does happen, it's such a kindness.

Even more powerful is that I was able to live in a state of peace because humility was my guide. There was peace through the loss of a relationship and the establishment of boundaries. There was peace as God restored and reconciled a relationship.

"Where there is humility, there is peace."

CREATE STRUCTURE FOR SAFETY, STRENGTH, AND PEACE

In the ancient world, cities ensured peace for their citizens by building walls that surrounded them. Two aspects of every wall were crucial to the long-term health and stability of the city: a gate and a watchtower.

Gates kept the people in the city safe and kept unsafe people out of the city. Watchtowers allowed people to look to the horizon and see whether their coming visitors would bring peace or disrupt peace and bring war.

If a city had no gate to let people in or out, people would become isolated and risk not having crucial supplies. If a city had no watchtower, people would be unable to see what was happening outside their walls and would be more vulnerable to surprise attacks from their enemies. A city needed both a gate and a watchtower to be strong and safe.

I've come to think of humility as a gate and the need to protect our hearts and keep watch over our relationships as a watchtower.

A city wall without a gate is actually a prison. If we construct boundaries without humility, we are constructing a prison of isolation that will only hurt us in the long run.

A city without a watchtower will always be caught off guard. Boundaries without humble awareness will involve limits that don't actually meet the needs of people's hearts and protect them.

So, how about a recap?

Humility prevents us from not having any boundaries, and if we don't have boundaries, everyone can get in and rob us of our peace and solitude.

Humility protects us from constructing barriers that isolate us and reject others.

It keeps us aware of whether our relationships are bringing peace or robbing us of peace.

And another key idea to keep in mind: Humility is not an invitation to be hurt, stepped on, or taken advantage of. When we allow our humility to be the source of confidence and courage to establish appropriate boundaries, we protect ourselves and others for a greater good—the possibility of peace. This is the blessing of living with wise boundaries from a humble heart.

> **HUMILITY IS NOT AN INVITATION TO BE HURT, STEPPED ON, OR TAKEN ADVANTAGE OF.**

The other day I was working in my home study when Britt yelled, "Joey, you've got to come see what EmJ just did!"

Now, this is pretty common. Our three-year-old, EmJ, does cute things almost constantly.

I walked into the kitchen and Britt was holding EmJ, who had a big grin on her face and a bunch of random stuff in her arms. Britt had wanted to see what EmJ would do if Britt just kept handing her stuff, and she captured her response on video.

EmJ was happy to hold the first few items. When her hands were full, Britt kept adding more stuff and EmJ started dropping some things. Looking down, she said, "Oh no . . . Full."

EmJ managed to hold a few more items as they kept coming at her, then finally, exhausted, she looked at Britt and said frankly, "I can't do it. No more."

I was floored. It was so cute but also a super valuable lesson. EmJ loved her mom but could no longer do what her mom was asking her to do, so she communicated that. "I can't do it." She put up a limit, and she was firm: "No more."

EmJ exercised humble boundaries. She knew who she was. She knew what she was and was not capable of. She accepted that she would have to tell her mom that she couldn't do something. Then, in a loving but honest way, she simply established the boundary by saying, "No more." And when Britt tried to give her another item, EmJ put her hands up and shook her head no.

> LET'S PUT HUMILITY TO WORK TO NURTURE HEARTS AND RELATIONSHIPS, MAKING THEM SAFE AND STRONG AND FULL OF PEACE.

Friends, a three-year-old can do this. And this is such good news, because it's a great indication that you and I can do it too.

How about we decide here and now to have a marked moment? We can make a decision to move forward in new ways. But here is what it will take.

Let's stop hesitating and overthinking boundaries.

Let's set out to be firm and kind, honest and loving, wise and caring.

Let's put humility to work to nurture hearts and relationships, making them safe and strong and full of peace.

CHAPTER 15

WHEN BAD THINGS HAPPEN TO HUMBLE PEOPLE

A FEW DAYS before Thanksgiving one year, I was busy trying to wrap up a few work projects so our family could hit the road and head to my uncle's house in Houston, just like we do every year. When I saw that my mom had texted, I anticipated the usual *When are you leaving?* or *What do the kids want to eat?* But instead it read, *Ruthie is missing. Please pray for her to be found.*

My mom and Ruthie's mom, Vinaya, are best friends. Our families are very close, so much so that I call Ruthie's mom Vinaya Aunty and would often lovingly refer to Ruthie and her sisters as my "cousins." Ruthie was in college, so I figured she may have just overslept and Vinaya Aunty and my mom were being overanxious.

A few hours later, I looked down at my phone and was paralyzed by mom's next text.

They found Ruthie's body.

Ruthie had been just nineteen years old. She'd been heading back to her home on campus after a mentoring event. As she walked toward her car in a parking garage, a man catcalled her. Ruthie ignored him and went on her way. Then the man followed her into the garage and murdered her.[1]

The shocking story ended up making national and international news. It left a family and an entire Indian community in Chicago utterly devastated.

Ruthie was the best of people. She was innocent and active in her local church. She loved her sisters and brother. She was her momma's shadow; wherever Vinaya Aunty went, Ruthie was there. When I think of humble confidence, I think of my sweet "cousin" Ruthie. Why did such a horrible thing happen to such a beloved, humble girl and her family?

"It's just not fair."

That's a phrase I hear often.

It's one I say too.

It's not fair when people get hurt. It's not fair when people get sick. It's not fair when someone loses a loved one or watches them suffer.

"It just doesn't make any sense."

That's another phrase we say. And rightly so. It makes no sense when bad things happen. It makes even less sense when bad things happen to humble people.

When bad things happen to humble people, it can leave us wondering, *Was humility even worth it?* I think this is a fair and honest question.

Before we try to answer it, we need to reflect on what we think humility will offer us. At some level (subconscious or conscious), we've come to believe that good things should happen to good people and bad things should happen to bad people. People who practice humility would fall in the "good" category, so when bad things happen to them, our entire system for understanding good and bad falls apart.

This way of thinking actually aligns with ancient ideologies and the mindsets of people from the biblical time period. It is known as "retributional theology," meaning if you sinned, you would suffer. So if you were experiencing suffering, it was evident you had been sinning. In today's world we probably don't refer to it as *sin* but instead as simply doing things that lack morality.

Honestly, I think we just want to try to make sense of suffering.

It's much easier to rationalize the hurt and heartache people endure if we can associate it with some kind of wrongdoing. *Well, they kind of deserved it*, we can think, and then feel lighter. All of this goes out the window when the hurt individual is good, acting honorably and exuding kindness and love. How can it be okay for these humble people to hurt when they've done so much good?

A HUMILITY-DRIVEN LIFE

One such person was the great German theologian and pastor Dietrich Bonhoeffer. He is most famously known for his active resistance against the Nazis, including his part in a failed assassination attempt on Hitler. I try to read a few biographies every year, and one of my favorites is Charles Marsh's *Strange Glory: A Life of Dietrich Bonhoeffer*. It is more critical in nature and examines Bonhoeffer's life through primary resources—his letters, his journal entries, firsthand accounts of those closest to him.

Bonhoeffer grew up in an upper-middle-class family, descending from doctors, judges, professors, artists, musicians—prominent members of German society. His grandmother was a countess. While Bonhoeffer's family experienced privilege due to their social status and wealth, they also deeply valued compassion and generosity. His mother especially exemplified this as she helped less fortunate people who were viewed as outsiders. His family had, in a sense, power, stability, and control, yet his parents taught him the power of humble kindness.

As an adult, Bonhoeffer's combined intelligence, talent, and privilege provided every opportunity for him to move into positions of power. Instead, he took "what for a young man of his ambition and talent was a path of profound humility. We see in Bonhoeffer's career, in fact, a movement from the center to the margins of society that counters our assumptions about the trajectory of a gifted life."[2]

Bonhoeffer didn't follow the promises of pride and chase after more money, power, or control. Instead, his humility drove him to fully devote himself to studying, teaching, and living out the truth of Jesus.

When Nazi forces began taking over German society, Bonhoeffer courageously pushed against them. He stood firm in his knowledge of the God who reigned above earthly leaders, of his own God-given worth, and of the value of all image bearers, both Jews and non-Jews. For the sake of others, he allowed himself to become a target of a ruthless, diabolical regime.

Bonhoeffer's resistance eventually culminated in an arrest, incarceration, and a death sentence. Yet even on the road to meet his end at a Nazi prison, humility continued to be his guiding compass.

A fellow prisoner reported, "Bonhoeffer was all humility and sweetness; he always seemed to me to diffuse an atmosphere of happiness, of joy in every smallest event in life, and of deep gratitude for the mere fact that he was alive . . . He was one of the very few men I have ever met to whom his God was real and ever close to him."[3]

Someone else remarked that Bonhoeffer "did a great deal to

keep some of the weaker brethren from depression and anxiety," including an atheist.[4] The fact that he showed equal love, care, and compassion to all people, regardless of their differences from him, is a testament to his high view of human dignity.

Now comes the part I struggle with.

What I want to write, what I wish were true, is that the war ended days before Bonhoeffer's scheduled execution. That the records show he was saved at the eleventh hour—proving that good things will always happen to humble people.

But that was not the case for Bonhoeffer. Bad things happened to this very humble pastor.

The descriptions of Bonhoeffer's execution are horrific. Getting stripped naked. Having his arms tied behind him. Being hung on a hook like "animals in a slaughterhouse," cruelly designed to extend suffering.

I can't help but think of how his experience mirrored the Roman method of crucifixion. Both involved being hung. Both aimed to prolong death as long as possible. Both intended to completely humiliate the person and strike fear into everyone else. I have a feeling Bonhoeffer may have made the same connection.

And yet, do you know what Bonhoeffer said before heading into this nightmare?

"This is the end. For me, the beginning of life."[5]

The path of humiliation in this world was the entrance into honor and Jesus' presence in heaven.

We started this chapter talking about the concept of retributional theology. We acknowledged that deep down we all have the feeling that good things should happen to humble people, and when that doesn't happen, we can't help but question if humility is actually worth prioritizing.

Now would be a good time to remind ourselves what humility is not.

Humility is not an ace card that gets us out of hard or impossible situations.

Humility is not a guaranteed escape from bad things happening to us.

Humility will not prevent us from experiencing fear.

If this is what we think humility will provide for us, we will be frustrated. We'll get incredibly angry. It may cause us to shut down, lean further into self-protection, or reject humility altogether.

If we try to force humility to give us what we want instead of what God wants, we are not only weaponizing it for our own agenda but also cutting ourselves off from the benefits God intends for us.

THE COURAGE FOR EVERY HARD THING

Let's go back to Bonhoeffer's final moments. Why didn't he ever get to the point of rejecting God for allowing him to suffer and just forgetting his whole Christ-focused ethic for life? Why didn't he cut a deal with the Nazis, agreeing to spill intel secrets on the resistance in exchange for his life? What kept him on a steady path of confidence and courage?

I tend to think it was because he'd spent years cultivating a humble heart.

Humility gave Bonhoeffer the confidence to face his fears and the courage to walk through hurt—including that final walk to the gallows for an hours-long execution.

Here's why.

First, humility brought Bonhoeffer's focus to the cross of Christ, not to the gallows. His entire adult life revolved around discussing Jesus' life, death, and resurrection. He frequently contemplated

Jesus' suffering. In his famous classic, *The Cost of Discipleship*, Bonhoeffer wrote, "The yoke and the burden of Christ are His cross."[6]

Humility shifts our perspective from the small world of self to the vast world of God. It opens our eyes to his grandeur and reminds us that nothing we walk through is void of his presence. We become God-focused people instead of self-focused people.

> HUMILITY SHIFTS OUR PERSPECTIVE FROM THE SMALL WORLD OF SELF TO THE VAST WORLD OF GOD.

Second, humility reminded Bonhoeffer of who he was in light of who God is. He was a child of God, cherished and loved by God. This reminder of his dignity and worth undoubtedly sustained him throughout all the difficult situations he faced.

Third, humility helped Bonhoeffer locate himself in the community of God, even when he experienced solitude in prison or isolation. In his loneliest moment he was never truly alone, because believers are always connected to each other and to Christ. Bonhoeffer once wrote, "In Christ mankind is really drawn into communion with God, just as in Adam mankind fell."[7] Bonhoeffer understood that to be in communion with God was to be firmly established in the family of God.

Even as you and I have moments of being physically alone, we are always spiritually knit together with God's family and connected through the Holy Spirit.

So, considering Bonhoeffer, what do we do when bad things happen to humble people? I think we recall these truths:

1. There is a God who is bigger than every situation we face.
2. This God loves us; he cares for us; and he proved it by sending his Son to us, to be with us through the indwelling Holy Spirit.

3. God has formed a new family that we belong to. We are never alone, because we belong to the family of God.

4. The suffering we experience, whether it is placed on us by others or is a result of our humble obedience, unites us to Jesus. As we remember this, it will shape our own understanding and acceptance of suffering in our lives.

THE KIND OF SUFFERING THAT COMES OUT OF NOWHERE

Bonhoeffer knew exactly why he was in such a tragic situation. His choices, driven by his ethics and moral conscience, essentially led him to it. But what about the situations where bad things happen to good, humble people and there are no explanations for them?

There's a story in the Old Testament that will help us here. Long before Bonhoeffer found himself in a prison cell, a humble and upright man named Job went through the unthinkable.

The book of Job opens like a movie, showing a behind-the-scenes look at God in his heavenly throne room, the King in his royal court. Angels are there with him, along with Satan—or "the Satan," as we see in the Hebrew *ha-satan*. The definite article ("the") indicates this was a title of a supernatural being who had the job of accusing humans.[8] In fact, the Hebrew *satan* can also be translated as "adversary."

After Satan told God he'd been roaming the globe (looking for people to accuse, no doubt), God asked, "Have you considered my servant Job? No one else on earth is like him, a man of perfect integrity, who fears God and turns away from evil" (Job 1:8).

This is one glowing report! God vouched for Job's strong faith and good character, and described Job as *his own* servant, showing a personal connection between them. If Job could have heard God say this, I bet it'd have been the highlight of his life!

I love what one commentator wrote about this verse: "Job is God's boast."[9]

Press pause on Job's story for a minute. I want to tell you something.

It's something I hope you'll let settle into your soul.

What God said about Job is what he says about *you*. This very minute, God feels this way about you, because you are rooted in Christ Jesus.

Right now I want to ask you to do something that may feel a bit silly but is so worth it.

Repeat this after me: "[Insert your name] is God's boast."

I know, weird, right?

Try it again. Let it get less weird.

"[Insert your name] is God's boast."

It is absolutely, seriously true. *God thinks much of you.* He loves you. He values you. You are truly his boast! And if you need a qualifier or reminder of how this can be true, just look back at the cross. The precious Son of God hung on a tree so you and I could become children of God.

All right. Back to Job.

God was proud of him, no doubt about it. But that didn't stop God from presenting Job as an option for the adversary and allowing Satan to pile up tragedies in Job's life.

I've got to say, this is a really hard part of the text.

If Job was a man of integrity (meaning he was upright and moral in his actions), how could anything bad happen to him? We're all asking this. But the fact that our minds go there is evidence of the "good people = good things" belief lingering in us.

While there is mystery around these issues, I want us to remember something we can be sure of: nothing ever happened to Job without God being right there with him, even if Job couldn't see or feel him. Whatever happened, Job's good, powerful God would be bigger than what he faced and would be able to sustain him.

There's something you should know about Job before we continue: He struggled with fear. (We're with you, Job.) Later in his story, in response to a personal disaster, he said, "The thing *I feared* has overtaken me, and what I dreaded has happened to me" (3:25).

He was a bit of a helicopter parent, worrying about his kids a lot and getting overinvolved in their issues (he needed to read that chapter about boundaries). After his kids would party, Job would offer burnt offerings to God on their behalf, thinking, "Perhaps my children have sinned, having cursed God in their hearts" (1:5).[10] He believed if his children sinned, they'd be punished, and his fear of that punishment drove him to offer these just-in-case sacrifices for them.

Well, it wasn't long before Satan unleashed havoc onto Job's life, causing physical pain, property losses, and—most crushing of all—the death of his children. All he'd worked for, all he'd cherished, was suddenly *gone*. Job faced the horrors of both seeing his fears come true and feeling the pain of their reality.

What do we do when the fear of what might happen meets the pain of what has happened?

In later chapters we see Job run the gamut of emotions—agony, anger, despair; he felt all his intense feelings and asked all his hard questions. We can see our own humanness in him. But his initial response was one of absolute trust in God: "Naked I came from my mother's womb, and naked I will leave this life. The LORD gives, and the LORD takes away. Blessed be the name of the LORD" (1:21). It's a stunning response, one truly from a heart of humility.

But does the fact that Job was humble, upright, and good mean he would let people walk all over him and accuse him of things he didn't do?

No! I've got to say, I find Job's choices in this next part so encouraging.

While Job was still in the thick of trauma, Job's friends came for a visit and brought their retributional theology with them. They searched for a hidden fault or sin in Job; clearly, he had done something evil in order to experience this level of divine calamity in his life. All he had to do was admit it—just confess, repent, and move on! But that would require Job to compromise his good character and integrity.

I love that Job told his dead-wrong friends, "I also have a mind like you; *I am not inferior to you.* Who doesn't know the things you are talking about?" (12:3). His humble confidence and courage led him to continually refute false accusations and eventually call out his friends for straight-up humiliating him (12; 19:3).

Job could, however, face that humiliation and walk through it, because humility was both his protection and preservation. Job consistently kept his heart and mind focused on what was true about God. This awareness kept him in a posture of humility, protecting him from giving into arrogant pride or shameful defeat.

"I DON'T KNOW, BUT YOU DO"

Toward the end of the book of Job, when God finally came on the scene and spoke to Job, we expect a divine *aha* moment. God will vindicate him, catch him up, and cheer him up. He'll explain the opening scene of Job 1, letting Job in on the cosmic situation he unknowingly found himself in. He'll congratulate Job for persevering without cursing or sinning against him.

But that's not what happened. God essentially told Job, "All right, you wanted to talk to me? Cool. Get ready, because I'm going to start telling you what you need to hear."

And, boy, did he. A monologue describing God's unsearchable power and sovereignty stretches across four chapters (38–41), with questions like "Where were you when I established the earth?" (38:4). "Do you have an arm like God's? Can you thunder with a voice like his?" (40:9).

To us, God's words to Job in these chapters can come across as harsh. But hidden in the text are elements of God's kind compassion and love for Job:

1. He referred to Job as "my servant" repeatedly (four times in Job 42:7–9) when speaking to one of Job's friends, something he never said about the friends. Job was *his*; their bond was made clear.

2. He phrased his questions to Job in an indirect way. He didn't say, "You were not there when I founded the earth." Instead, he used rhetorical questions ("Where were you . . . ?") to draw Job into the discussion and help him remember realities he may have been forgetting.[11]

3. In wisdom literature (which the book of Job is a part of), when a father asks rhetorical questions of a son, "the intent is not to humiliate but to help the student grow so that he can receive the blessings of wisdom."[12] The way God interacted with Job was meant to reinforce Job's already humble posture. Each question was meant to lead Job to simply and humbly say, "I don't know, but you do, Lord."[13]

Okay, I'm going to repeat that one.
I don't know, but you do, Lord.
This may be one of the most powerful responses we can train

our hearts to say when unexplainable bad things happen to us or our loved ones.

As I was writing this chapter, something horrible happened to one of the humblest people I know, my friend Pete. He looked like a legit Viking, but the gentlest Viking you would ever come across. Pete was diagnosed with stage-four colon cancer a few years ago, and he was incredibly open with the people in his life about his experience. The humility behind his transparency blew me away.

He fought and struggled for years, and the cancer continued to spread. So he and his family decided to transition him into hospice care. It was devastating news.

Our family sent him a video message letting him know we loved him and were praying for him, his wife, and his daughters. I had to explain what was going on to my kids, and when Levi realized this was most likely a goodbye, he broke down in tears. He kept saying, "It's not fair!"

Doing my very best to hold back my own tears, I could only think, *It's so not fair at all.*

In all honesty, none of it makes any sense to me. Why would something so horrible happen to such an honest and kind man?

Pete and I worked together for eight years, and during my most challenging and grueling times at work, he was the most faithful friend I could have asked for. He was always available to talk, process, and give the best advice. I'm really grateful I got to read this section of my book to Pete as he lay on his hospice bed next to his family. Pete passed just a month afterward. When I think of someone in my life who has exemplified humility, I think of Pete Heiniger.

As I've struggled to make sense of all this, I continually return to the feet of Jesus. I gaze upon him, and I whisper the only thing I can: "I don't know, but you do, Lord."

IT'S ALL ABOUT THE *WHO*, NOT THE *WHY*

I think we can learn from Job 38 to 41 that God will not always tell us the *why* behind bad things that happen to humble people. Rather, he will remind us of the *who* that is with humble people who face fears and walk through pain.

And this is a more significant gift for us than knowing why. You may have heard the phrase "More money, more problems." Well, I think it also could be said, "More knowledge, more questions." What we need more than knowledge about the inner workings of creation and how everything is held together is confidence in our God. The one who created and sustains all things, who is near the brokenhearted, who is utterly, thoroughly *good*.

> WHAT WE NEED MORE THAN KNOWLEDGE ABOUT THE INNER WORKINGS OF CREATION AND HOW EVERYTHING IS HELD TOGETHER IS CONFIDENCE IN OUR GOD.

The irony at the end of Job's story is that God affirmed Job in front of the friends who humiliated him. "I am angry with you," God said, "for you have not spoken the truth about me, as my servant Job has" (42:7). Their wrongs had to be made right, and it could be done only through Job offering prayer and sacrifices on their behalf (vv. 8–9). And so it was Job's humility that saved his friends from God's wrath (v. 7).

I think it is also interesting that it wasn't until after Job prayed for his friends that all his fortunes were restored and doubled (v. 10). I almost wonder if this was a last test of humility. Would Job's awareness of God, who he'd once heard of but now had seen, flow into him and out onto his friends? It would, and here we find a hidden and unexpected blessing that came through the stability and consistency of a humble heart. Peace was restored to Job and his friends.

Here's the surprising thing about the book of Job: We expect it to reveal why humans suffer, but it doesn't. It shows us how humans can *grow emotionally and spiritually* in the midst of suffering.

On my Instagram the other day, I invited responses to a simple fill-in-the-blank statement: "You are afraid of . . ." The answers were sobering. The ones that came up over and over were losing children, a spouse dying, life after a divorce, and being alone.

When any of these fears become a reality for humble people, it is always tragic and painful. Bad things do happen to humble people, and there is nothing on this side of eternity we can do to prevent that horrible consequence of sin that corrupted all creation.

But hardship for the humble is not an indictment against their character or righteousness. It is an avenue for God's grace to be known, to be uniquely experienced.

When the bad things come, instead of obsessing over *why* they have come, we can look to *who* is with us (Jesus) in the midst of them.

We can decide in advance that whenever we experience those bad things, our first response will be to pray, *God, I don't know, but you do.* As we make this prayer our predetermined response, we are in fact settling into the comfortable yoke that Jesus helps us carry as we walk through suffering.

I've often said that repetition in the Bible always has a reason. Part of that reason is to remind us of routine and rhythms that are intended to be seen, heard, and experienced as we read through the narrative of Scripture. The same can be said of a predetermined and repeated response that we practice in life.

Here is a suggestion for a routine you can repeat. As you lay your head down to sleep, whisper this simple prayer:

God, I don't know what tomorrow will bring, but you do.

Your presence next to me builds confidence within me.

In the midst of my hurt, let me see a bigger picture of your holiness and your gracious work in my life.

I know you are with me, God, so I will rest in the peace you give me. Keep steering your heart in that direction.

And keep holding on to this: humility is God's gift to you in every situation.

It helps you face your fears.

It connects you to the power and peace of God.

And it turns your unexplainable suffering into a means of transformation, deepening and strengthening you into maturity, as you trust and depend on him more and more.

THE ART OF STAYING HUMBLE

"OKAY, SO NOW I guess we just wash, rinse, and repeat?"

We had just finished recording an episode of the *Therapy &* *Theology* podcast series, and I was referring to how we'd approach the next recording.

As soon as I said it, Lysa and a bunch of my coworkers at Proverbs 31 Ministries chuckled.

This seemed to me an odd moment to laugh.

I asked them if I'd used the saying the wrong way or mixed a metaphor. I'm notorious for mixing metaphors.

Lysa, smiling, said, "No, you actually said it perfectly. We can just tell you've been working in women's ministry for a while based on the metaphors you use."

Jim looked at me with a grin and gave me a fist bump. I like to think that was his way of saying, *It's cool. You're still one of the guys.*

Wash. Rinse. Repeat.

I'm saying the same thing to you now that I said at the end of that recording session. It's perfect because it implies intentionality and daily action.

Yes, you've gained a lot of knowledge. But all this knowledge is intended to guide you into pursuing a life of humility. All this theology you've learned about humility is intended to be lived and embodied. As A. W. Tozer said, "Knowledge without humility is vanity."[1] And so the journey we've been taking in this book has led us to an exciting position: the ability to live out humility!

I would be heartbroken if, after you read this book, you considered humility to be a one-and-done kind of deal, something that you could work at, perfect, and move on from. So I'm going to say yet again: humility is the soil of the Christian life that needs to be constantly tended to. It's something you practice every day, which changes you a little bit more all the time, shaping you to be like Jesus.

Maybe you have that idea locked in, but part of you is still asking, *How do I do that, exactly?*

I think we all could use some tips and reminders going forward. Let's go over some practical ways we can continually cultivate humility and keep at this Jesus way of life.

THE EVERYDAY JESUS WAY

1. REMEMBER GOD'S PRESENCE AND CHARACTER.

First and always, we need to be aware of the presence and power of God in our lives. If we don't keep this central, everything else will fall out of focus.

It doesn't have to be super spiritual; it can be quite simple. Take a walk and when the sun hits your face, remember that God keeps that sun in its place. When we see creation in all its beauty, we are seeing evidence of God's creative power.

To be humble and stay humble, we need to see God. And when we see him, our response is to be in awe and reverence, a holy fear. We're not talking about a debilitating terror here. This is a holy awareness of just how great God is. It's the awestruck love we see in Psalm 33:8–9: "Let the whole earth fear the LORD; let all the inhabitants of the world stand in awe of him. For he spoke, and it came into being; he commanded, and it came into existence."

The blessings of peace and protection come from having this fear and reverence in our hearts (Malachi 2:5). The God who creates all things is the same one who sustains everything, including you and me.

If we want to continually cultivate humility, we need to continually turn our eyes to God and respond to him in reverence.

2. MAINTAIN SELF-AWARENESS.

The difference between self-awareness and self-obsession is humility. Pride distorts our self-awareness and spins us into instability. As John Stott said, "If pride and madness go together, so do humility and sanity."[2] The kind of self-awareness we're after is in tune with how much we need God and the fact that he meets all our needs.

In the same way a gardener may walk into her garden and check on the plants and soil, we need to keep checking on the soil of our hearts. Self-awareness connected to our awareness of God will help us continually return to a posture of humility.

3. BE ON GUARD AGAINST SIN.

Sin threatens humility at every turn. The corruption first shows up inside us, then works itself out of us. Some theologians have described it as the heart bending in upon itself, or "man turned in on himself."[3] When sin captures our heart, it makes us self-absorbed. When we are obsessed with ourselves, we will justify whatever it takes to make ourselves happy.

So we need to keep our eyes open and consistently check our hearts for the empty promises of sin. Once again, humility will help us with this. Humility is so much more than simply being struck by our sin. It is ultimately about being captivated by the majesty of God.

4. PRIORITIZE OTHERS.

Humility is meant to be lived out in community. When we rejoice, laugh, grieve, and process the hard and holy parts of life with others, we remind our hearts that life is about so much more than me, myself, and I. A daily commitment to building others up and considering what is good for them is good for our souls.

You are bound to see people you love succeed in areas of life you long to succeed in, and when you do, it can be disorienting. You want to cheer them on and shout how hyped you are for them, but inside, you can't escape the questions. *Why them and not me? What have I done to prevent good things like this happening in my life? How do I support them when what I see in them only highlights what I'm lacking?*

Humility leads us to process our emotions with God and then shift our focus. It helps us see that others' success doesn't equal our failure. Humility is God's gift that enables us to look beyond ourselves and into the greater good we can help establish in others. We can pursue helping those people we cherish become even better people. Our humility becomes the platform for someone else's greatness. This is something that is scorned by the world but celebrated in the kingdom of God.

It's possible that one of the most significant blessings we can experience is living out a daily practice of humility in relation to others. To do what scholar and pastor Eugene Peterson once said that humility enables us to do: to be "in relationship with other people without competing with them."[4]

5. BE COMMITTED TO THE PRACTICE OF HUMILITY.

We commit to things we believe in. We've seen how humility is the hidden piece to what we all long for—peace. We need to commit to it emotionally, physically, and spiritually. Commitment requires conviction. Conviction is impossible without really believing in the benefits and beauty of humility.

One of the benefits of humility is that it will give you the confidence to face your fears and the courage to walk through your hurts.

The beauty of humility is that it is the identity marker of what it means to be a Christian. It's the active agent that conforms us into the image of Jesus.

6. BE PERSISTENT.

Don't give up. I love what Teresa of Ávila once said: "Humility must always be doing its work like a bee making its honey in the hive: without humility all will be lost."[5] Yes, there will be setbacks. Yes, pride will show up in unexpected places. And yes, we will sin and compromise the soil of humility we've worked hard to cultivate. But friend: *Don't. Give. Up.* It's worth it.

Even better, God is with us, and his Holy Spirit will empower and equip us. When we sin, we can repent, confess, and return to the feet of Jesus. He will lift us up, exalt us, and send us on our way to continue living for him.

It may be imperfect, but it will always be a forward-moving process. We can accept this because perfection was never the goal.

7. BE WHO GOD CREATED YOU TO BE.

Embrace who God made you to be. Remember, you are a one-of-a-kind child of God, created to be unique. There is no need to try to be someone else. And what a great tragedy that would be, because there is only one you in all of human existence!

In order to be who God created you to be, commit to celebration and to cancel comparison. Simply be you—the steady, confident you. The you that exudes humility in compassion and grace. The you that establishes humble boundaries to bring out the best in you and others.

LIVE OUT WHAT YOU WERE MADE FOR

There are multiple payoffs of practicing humility—the confidence to face our fears; the strength to endure our struggles and pain; a powerful, soul-settling peace. But do you know what the ultimate payoff is? Regaining our true humanity, which God has always wanted for us.

Humility gives us the power to live out what we were made for. You and I were made to experience life in the family of God, which involves not only peace, safety, and stability but also the honor of representing God to the world.

Remember how Adam and Eve were considered royalty in Eden? God made them part of his royal family, and he does the same with us. When we live in his royal family, we have a royal responsibility: to serve as winsome witnesses of a different way of doing life, exuding peace to a world that is so desperate for it.

This is exactly what the apostle Paul was getting at when he wrote, "We are *ambassadors* for Christ, since God is making his appeal through us. We plead on Christ's behalf, 'Be reconciled to God.' He made the one who did not know sin to be sin for us, so that in him we might become the righteousness of God" (2 Corinthians 5:20–21).

The Greek word translated as "ambassador" here refers to a person who functions as a "representative of a ruling authority."[6]

In the ancient world, ambassadors

- were sent on special assignments;
- represented a ruling authority (or person); and
- acted with the authority of the sender.[7]

This is what you and I get to do. As ambassadors of Christ sent on a special assignment, we proclaim the goodness of the gospel to a world desperate for security, strength, and peace. We do this not in our own authority but as representatives of the King of the cosmos!

Remarkably, he not only sends us but also *comes with* us. Wherever we go, the power, authority, and presence of the King goes. We know this because he has sealed us with his very own Spirit as a guarantee and deposit that dwells inside us (Ephesians 1:13–14).

This doesn't mean the hard moments won't come. People will disregard us and insult us (just like people did with Jesus). This is why humility is so crucial in all of this. It helps us endure the hardships and persecutions, and all along the way, it is helping us establish our true humanity.

I recently went to India for a family trip. While I was there, I had to get some paperwork done at the US embassy. So I was a US citizen who was in India, and—this is insane—the moment I stepped onto the US embassy, which is located in India, I was no longer in India; I was back in America. But y'all . . . I was in India . . . *what?!*

This mirrors how we function as God's kingdom ambassadors, bringing the presence of one "country" into another. Wherever you and I go, the kingdom of God goes. Wherever we share the love of Jesus and exhibit the power of humble confidence, the people around us—our neighbors, friends, loved ones—are getting a taste of the goodness of God's kingdom and the peace available to them today.

Friend, when you and I live out daily humility, we are in fact advancing the kingdom of God in both tangible and intangible ways. Humility is indeed not a sign of our defeat but the mark of Christ's victory in our lives. Humility is what we get to carry with us, knowing we can face every fear and every hurt because we're united with him.

Welcome to the humble life. A life where you get to experience a beautiful harmony because you are

1. aware of the greatness and grandeur of God;
2. aware of your own value and worth; and
3. aware of the dignity of others.

You get to move through your days walking right beside Jesus, sharing his gentle yoke, wearing his humility clothes of victory and virtue. All the while being a visible witness to the greatness of the coming King and his kingdom!

The weaknesses, fears, and hurts—they're all still there. But they no longer crush you, because they are now an avenue to living in the power and strength of Jesus.

And in the most epic redemptive reversal, you become an avenue for others to experience the power and strength of Jesus.

Welcome to the Jesus way of life that gives us stability and steadiness.

Of confidence and courage.

Of peace in you, through you, and around you.

GETTING GROUNDED IN SCRIPTURAL HUMILITY

NOTHING WILL HELP us cultivate a life of humility quite like soaking our minds and hearts in the Scriptures. As we read through the Bible, we find humility everywhere. We find examples of humility, the lack of humility, and simple but profound words of wisdom that God wants us to have planted in our hearts.

As I was studying humility, I was struck by the sheer number of examples of it throughout Scripture and also how different each of them was from the others! Some were smack in the middle of the story of Israel. Others were songs the Israelites sang as a means of remembrance. Still others were wisdom sayings that parents and wise elders of a community would teach and display for the following generations to see. And then we have the New Testament's emphasis on humility, which Jesus lived out perfectly and Paul described as the defining mark of the Christian community.

I often found myself thinking, *I wish all these passages were gathered somewhere so I could come back to meditate on them more easily.* So that's why I put together this list of Bible verses we can study and reflect on as we cultivate humility in our lives.

I have also included a bite-size devotional thought for each passage. You can read the whole thing all the way through in one sitting, or you can use it as a devotional that daily steers your heart and mind toward humility.

1

> Moses and Aaron went in to Pharaoh and told him, "This is what the LORD, the God of the Hebrews, says: How long will you refuse to *humble* yourself before me? Let my people go, that they may worship me."
>
> —EXODUS 10:3

CONSIDER

Have you ever wondered, *What if Pharaoh had just listened to Moses? What if he hadn't merely acknowledged the God of Israel but actually submitted to the God of Israel as his king?* Imagine the countless lives that could have been saved. Pharaoh's own personal suffering would have been eased.

But instead, Pharaoh refused to humble himself before the Lord. Why? Because there was a disconnect between what he saw of God and what he believed about himself. The Egyptian religion believed that the pharaoh was the child of the gods and the physical representation of the gods of Egypt on earth. In other words, Pharaoh believed he himself was God.

Pharaoh is a powerful example of how important it is to allow our view of God to rightly inform how we view ourselves. Pharaoh refused to see himself in light of the greatness of God because that would require him to submit to God. His pride was deeply connected to idolatry.

Today is a great day to allow the question that was asked of Pharaoh to be asked of us. Friend, how long will you refuse (either actively or passively) to humble yourself before God?

CULTIVATE

Allow the following truths about your identity to be anchors for how you view yourself in light of God. In your quiet time with the Lord, read these verses. Consider writing them down. Say them to yourself:

- I am a child of God. (Romans 8:16–17)
- I am a reflection of God on earth because the Holy Spirit dwells inside me. (2 Corinthians 1:22)
- I have been given the great honor and responsibility to reflect the humility of Jesus to the world. (Ephesians 5:1)

COMMIT

Make a personal commitment today to participate in daily humility.

2

Remember that the LORD your God led you on the entire journey these forty years in the wilderness, so that he might *humble* you *and test you to know what was in your heart*, whether or not you would keep his commands. He *humbled* you by letting you go hungry; then he gave you manna to eat, which you and your ancestors had not known, so that you might learn that man does not live on bread alone but on every word that comes from the mouth of the LORD. Your clothing did not wear out, and your feet did not swell these forty years. Keep in mind that the LORD your God has been disciplining you just as a man disciplines his son.

—DEUTERONOMY 8:2–5

CONSIDER

In these verses, Moses reminded the Israelites of their trials to elicit their thankfulness in a faithful God, to remind them how he'd carried them through every hardship. And here we see one of the most neglected biblical practices: remembrance.

God had allowed trials and led Israel through the wilderness to expose what was in their hearts and lead them into a lifestyle of humility. Right at a moment when Israel thought all would be lost, they received manna to eat—they experienced the faithfulness of God.

Manna was something brand-new to them, something their "ancestors had not known" (Deuteronomy 8:16). It would have surprised—even shocked—them. Recalling that experience would have been a reminder that God works in ways beyond our imagination.

CULTIVATE

The trials of your life are not meaningless. You can learn from Israel that your trials and tribulations are moments to remember God's faithfulness and, in doing so, be led into humility.

Trials and hardships expose your weakness. And your weakness is the perfect place for humility to grow as you learn to rely on the one who is truly strong and able.

COMMIT

Today, practice a theology of remembrance. Recall one moment of hardship and write down how it led you to humility. Thank God for his faithfulness in and through it.

3

The LORD brings poverty and gives wealth; he humbles and he exalts. He raises the poor from the dust and lifts the needy from the trash heap. He seats them with noblemen and gives them a throne of honor. For the foundations of the earth are the LORD's; he has set the world on them. He guards the steps of his faithful ones, but the wicked perish in darkness, for a person does not prevail by his own strength.

—1 SAMUEL 2:7–9

CONSIDER

There is nothing in this world that takes place outside of the control of God. Your wealth is given to you by God. The question is, what will the wealth do to your heart?

The losses in your life were allowed by God for a reason. The question is, how will loss impact the condition of your heart? Will it make it hard and brittle, or will it remind you of your need for God?

The good news is that for children of God, loss and weakness are never permanent. God will intervene. The prophet Samuel said that God will lift up the poor and raise them with the noble. He will seat them on a throne of honor! We can be sure of this because he is the same God who owns the very foundations of the earth.

CULTIVATE

When good things happen in your life, how do those things cultivate thankfulness in your heart for God?

A heart that is humble is postured "low," even in the midst of success and riches. This heart posture places you in the perfect position for God to lift you up.

Similarly, when hard things happen, how can you remind yourself that hardship is not evidence of God's absence but the opportunity to lean closer into his presence?

COMMIT

Make the decision today to filter everything good and everything hard through a humble heart that always turns to God.

4

LORD, you have heard the desire of the humble;
you will strengthen their hearts.
You will listen carefully.

—PSALM 10:17

CONSIDER

God is not an absentee father. If you've never heard this before, I want to say it to you now: Your prayers and cries do not fall on deaf ears. Your tears are not spilled in front of a God who has turned his back on you.

In Psalm 10:17 the context of "the humble" is affliction and oppression. Essentially, bad things have been happening to good people. The psalmist's response to that shows us how we can respond to hardship while maintaining humility. It's about confidence, not questioning.

Notice the words in verse 17. It's not, "Will you please hear?" It is, "You have heard." It's an expression of confidence in the God who hears the desires of the humble and won't stop at just "hearing." He strengthens our hearts in preparation for whatever may come.

Notice the resolve isn't about the ease or removal of fear, pain, or hurt. Rather, it is a firmness in heart to endure and walk through hardship.

CULTIVATE

What is your default belief about God when bad things happen to you? Does this response come from a place of questioning or confidence?

What if you made the resolve today to be confident in the caring nature of God? You can make the psalmist's confidence your conviction—God hears and God acts.

The verse right before this one, Psalm 10:16, gives us an important detail about who God is: he is "King forever and ever." Our confidence is not without basis! It is rooted in the kingship of the Creator of heaven and earth.

COMMIT

Train your heart to respond to hardships from a place of confidence in King Jesus.

5

> Though the LORD is exalted,
> he takes note of the humble;
> but he knows the haughty from a distance.
> —PSALM 138:6

CONSIDER

To say that the Lord is "exalted" is a symbolic expression to refer to his glory and honor. To be exalted is to be placed in a position of favor, power, and authority. This is the place of God—exalted.

Typically, the higher the exaltation, the less need there would be to associate with the lowly. But our God is different. In his high place he "takes note," or he considers, the humble. What a blessing of humility! It puts us in plain purview of the exalted King of heaven who comes near to us.

In contrast, God also observes the "haughty" or prideful. In response to this, God keeps his distance. The nearness of God is not a guarantee. There are things that we can do or participate in that keep God at a distance.

CULTIVATE

You can be in danger of taking for granted the nearness of God if you fail to reflect on the exaltation of God. God is not like us; he is totally other. God is not created; he is the uncreated, eternally existing, all-powerful God.

When you cultivate this vision of God in your heart and mind, you position yourself below him. There you can benefit from the full impact and power of his awareness of the humble.

COMMIT

When you think of God, think of him first and foremost as King of the cosmos. Then, everything else that is true about him (his love, care, kindness, compassion, mercy, justice) will flow from his kingship, which reminds us of how great a blessing it is to be his children.

6

A person's pride will humble him,
but a humble spirit will gain honor.
—Proverbs 29:23

CONSIDER

Humility is not an option. We will all experience humility one way or another. The question is how we get to that place.

Pride's path of humility is humiliation. Pride can be defined as an unwarranted and overly elevated self-perspective. An exaggerated view of self is unhealthy and unhelpful.

Old Testament scholar Derek Kidner said it this way: "The special evil of pride is that it opposes the first principle of wisdom (the fear of the Lord) and the two great commandments."[1]

In the moment, it may seem like pride is paying off. But as Proverbs says, the only thing that pride pays off on is humiliation.

The posture of our hearts matters. A posture of pride will eventually produce humiliation. A posture of humility will provide honor.

CULTIVATE

The way you fight pride is through awe and reverence, or holy fear, of God. It is incredibly difficult to think too much of yourself when you are consumed with thinking about the greatness and glory of God.

It is a beautiful thing to consider that the path to honor is through humility. Take a moment to write down all the things that tempt you into pride (success, money, relationships). Next to each one of those things, write down how God has provided those things for you.

As you do this, you continually return to the source of all the good you have. This cultivates a "humble spirit."

COMMIT

Continually recall the way God has provided for you. Fight pride through worship.

The fear of mankind is a snare,
but the one who trusts in the LORD is protected.

—PROVERBS 29:25

CONSIDER

Fear can truly be debilitating. I once heard an analyst in a sports interview discuss the difference between "slow mortality" and "fast mortality." You can probably guess what this means: a slow or prolonged death, or a fast, quick, and unexpected death.[2] I think the same concept can be applied to fear. There can be a "slow fear" and a "fast fear." The slow fear works behind the scenes but actively over a long period of time. The fast fear shocks and paralyzes in a moment.

Proverbs 29:25 describes how these two types of fears can actually work together. The image of a "snare" brings to mind a strategic way of capture. The best snares are set where you least expect them. They are along a path an animal often travels, yet they're perfectly hidden. Then one day the animal steps on the snare and it's caught. For the animal, it feels like a total surprise and they are caught off guard. For the hunter who set the snare, it was patient and calculated work. The snare is "slow" as a hunter waits for it to be used, but it is fast and deadly when it is triggered.

Human fear is a trap set in subtlety. But there is hope for the one who trusts in the Lord. They are free from the entrapment of the snare because they are protected by the King.

CULTIVATE

Snares will always be present. Fear will always be a reality. But so is the assurance that God will always be with us. Read Proverbs 29:25 in light of Proverbs 18:10: "The name of the LORD is a strong tower;

the righteous run to it and are protected." If snares are typically on the ground, being lifted high is a safety.

That's what is promised for the humble. They run into the strong tower (the name of the Lord) and find safety. The Hebrew verb *nisgab*, translated as "protected" in Proverbs 18:10, has connotations of height and the security that comes with it.[3]

Where are you running? Creating rhythms and patterns of constantly running to God is an investment in the safety and security you long for.

COMMIT

Pray this simple prayer today: *Lord, I know the Enemy has snares set for me. But there is never a snare that can get in the way of your presence and protection. Today I am making the decision to turn to you and run safely into your arms. The snare may snare me, but you are my rescue.*

8

Seek the LORD, all you humble of the earth,
who carry out what he commands.
Seek righteousness, seek humility;
perhaps you will be concealed
on the day of the LORD's anger.
—ZEPHANIAH 2:3

CONSIDER

We search for things that have value. The more value and worth, the harder the search.

If you want to see our family go into a frantic search, just lose the Apple TV remote. That little remote holds immense value to our children, so when it's lost, it's time for full-on search mode. The

Apple TV remote brings satisfaction through a sense of control. With it you can turn on your favorite show and turn up or turn down the volume.

Herein lies a motivation. We seek what we believe will bring satisfaction.

The prophet Zephaniah told us to "seek" the Lord. When we participate in this search, it's an indication of humility. We don't seek aimlessly; our searching is focused on righteousness and an ongoing pursuit of humility.

CULTIVATE

We all search for things in our lives. I frequently search for a pen or my car keys. But the level of value and worth we place on the object of our search determines the depths to which we will be committed to finding it.

The car keys are vital for me, so I'll tear up the house to find them. A pen is helpful but not necessary. I can always take those car keys and run to Target to buy some new pens. I look for the pens half-heartedly. But I seek after those car keys with total commitment to finding them.

Half-hearted seeking after God is an indication of half-hearted adoration of God. Adoration is what flows from our hearts and toward God because we are truly aware of who he is.

Take some time today to intentionally seek after God. Take a walk and, as the sun hits your face, reflect on the Creator and sustainer of the sun. Step out onto your grass with bare feet. As you feel the grass and soil under your feet, remind yourself of the God who grants this stability.

COMMIT

Make an intentional decision to do an activity while reflecting on the presence of God in that space (taking a walk, standing barefoot on the grass, thirty seconds of intentional breathing, ten minutes of Scripture reading). In doing this, you are actually seeking after him.

9

> You have given me the shield of your salvation;
> your right hand upholds me,
> and your humility exalts me.
> You make a spacious place beneath me for my
> steps,
> and my ankles do not give way.
> —Psalm 18:35–36

CONSIDER

Earlier in Psalm 18, David referred to Yahweh as a shield (v. 30). Here in verse 35 he said that Yahweh gave him the shield of his salvation. In other words, Yahweh gave David *himself* as a source of protection and defense.

A shield was primarily a defensive weapon. When a soldier raised it up, it protected him from an enemy's offensive attacks. Hiding behind a shield wasn't a sign of weakness. It was a gesture of humility that allowed the soldier to acknowledge he was being attacked, to protect himself, and to gather himself to go on the offensive.

The phrase "your right hand" is often used throughout the Old Testament to reference the power, strength, and authority of God (Isaiah 41:13; Psalm 89:13).

The movement in these verses from the Psalms is important. God gives us a shield (himself) that saves, and he doesn't expect us to save ourselves. Rather, "his right hand" finishes what he set out. God does what he didn't have to do; he exalts and lifts us up!

CULTIVATE

Sometimes it can feel like you need to save yourself. David's words remind us that we are passive participants in the action of God. It's not that you are without responsibility, but you are to be faithful to do what God asks of you, and sometimes that is to humbly sit back and allow him to do what only he can do.

This kind of humility takes practice. It is an art that needs to be worked on over a period of time. It can be lost and forgotten if not attended to.

In your journal or Notes app, write down things you have been holding on to or trying to achieve that are beyond your control. Next to each of these things, write out your heart's desire.

COMMIT

This week, return to the list you just made and pray this simple prayer: *God, I recognize and admit I don't have control over everything. But I know you do. So I ask for your help, your strength, and your wisdom. God, I'll be responsible for what I can be. And I will trust you for everything else.*

10

He told a parable to those who were invited, when he noticed how they would choose the best places for themselves: "When you are invited by someone to a wedding banquet, don't sit in the place of honor, because a more distinguished person than you may have been invited by your host. The one who invited both of you may come and say to you, 'Give your place to this man,' and then in humiliation, you will proceed to take the lowest place.

"But when you are invited, go and sit in the lowest

place, so that when the one who invited you comes, he will say to you, 'Friend, move up higher.' You will then be honored in the presence of all the other guests. For everyone who exalts himself will be humbled, and the one who humbles himself will be exalted."

—LUKE 14:7–11

CONSIDER

Presumption is a dangerous trait. To presume something is to believe something is true but not know for sure. In the case of the parable in Luke 14, the presumption is of importance. The idea that no one else that will come to this wedding is more important.

The problem with presumption is that it's intimately connected to pride, or an overindulged view of yourself. When this happens, humiliation follows.

But notice the other approach. It's not self-degrading, but it's an honest awareness that someone more important could come. Better to take a seat of less honor, just in case someone comes looking for their seat and you are in it.

What's interesting is that both perspectives are presumptive in nature. The difference between pride and humility is the object of that presumption—yourself (pride) or others (humility).

Jesus taught that Scripture's repeated message is that the humble will be exalted. God will come into a room, see you sitting contentedly at the back, and insist on moving you to the front. We have no need to exalt ourselves through pride, because we have a loving God who exalts the humble.

CULTIVATE

Presumption isn't necessarily a negative thing; it depends on what you are presuming. This parable teaches us to develop a type of presumption that considers others and makes room for their honor.

In doing so, you do something in your heart that sets a rhythm of perspectives. You learn to see the world not through the lens of "me, myself, and I" but in consideration of others.

Developing this may be easier and more practical than we want to admit. Next time you're out shopping, make the intentional decision to let someone who has a few items compared to your many items go in front of you at checkout. Maybe even let the person with a lot of items compared to your few items go in front of you also!

There are endless opportunities to consider others before yourself. Make it a practice now to develop the rich and fruitful soil of humility in your life.

COMMIT

Pick two ways you can be presumptive about others over yourself. Make the decision to practice these actions and then share your experience with a close friend. Tell them what you loved about it. Tell them also what you hated about it. Remember, humility and honesty always belong together.

11

A person should think of us in this way: as servants of Christ and managers of the mysteries of God.
—1 CORINTHIANS 4:1

CONSIDER

We have a rule in our house. If you cook, you don't clean. If Britt cooks, the kids and I all clean up. Yep, even my three-year-old daughter, EmJ. She wipes down tables and it's the cutest thing you've ever seen.

Households have rules, responsibilities, and expectations. Without them things would be chaotic. I always love to see my kids take real pride (the good kind) in responsibility at home. Why? Because they've realized that what they do and how they take care of the house is a reflection of who they are.

In 1 Corinthians 4:1 Paul said that the outside world should view us as "servants" of Jesus and "managers" of the mysteries of God. The Greek word translated as "managers" (*oikonomos*) is a word that describes an administrator, often of a household. Paul was saying we should remember that we are in fact members of God's household and we have the responsibility to steward the "mysteries of God." The mystery of God is the good work of Jesus on the cross. It's an invitation to every nation, tongue, and tribe to come and join Jesus to be included in this family.

To be a good steward or household manager, we have to remember first and foremost who the head of the household is. Without this, we could start to act in ways that go against what God wants and instead reflect what we want.

CULTIVATE

One of the ways you can strive toward being a good manager of the house of God is to remember the values and ethics of the family of God. God desires for his image bearers to worship him. He also desires unity and peace within the family.

One of the ways you can help accomplish unity and peace is to take the "low way." It's unnatural, but without it, unity and peace are next to impossible. Remember, taking the low way is not an invitation to allow others to hurt you, mistreat you, or take advantage of you. It is an invitation to consider others before yourself—to let someone else go first when you could have. As you build these practices into your life, your unity and peace serve as witness to the world of your love, kindness, and compassion, which is an essential mark of the family of God. It is an invitation to the world to partake in the "mysteries of God."

COMMIT

Like the people in every household, we need to know what our responsibilities are and what they are not. Write down three things you can be responsible for (for example, to share your story of God's kindness with a friend, to pray for someone in need, to allow someone else to go first when you could have).

In the coming days, do what is on your list to the best of your ability.

At the end of the week, write down what you learned about yourself in the process.

12

I, the prisoner in the Lord, urge you to walk worthy of the calling you have received, with all humility and gentleness, with patience, bearing with one another in love, making every effort to keep the unity of the Spirit through the bond of peace.

—Ephesians 4:1–3

CONSIDER

Something that really makes us aware of our limits and inability is when we are stuck: stuck in a room, stuck in a situation, stuck with a problem. It really doesn't matter what the context of the "stuck" is, it reminds us of our innate weakness.

So when Paul referred to himself as being a "prisoner in the Lord," every person in the church at Ephesus would have tilted their head, wondering, *Huh? Did he just say that?*

Yes, he did.

Paul was using a powerful word to describe how we should view ourselves in light of God. As a prisoner of the Lord, Paul submitted his will and desires to Jesus. This perspective helps us live out humility and gentleness.

Notice the goal: to keep unity through peace. How is this possible? By embodying a life of humility marked by gentleness. By exercising patience that enables us to relate to others in love.

The paradox of the kingdom of God is that as a "prisoner" of the Lord, we are actually the safest and freest we could ever be.

CULTIVATE

Take special note of the combination of humility and gentleness. This combination is used by Jesus (Matthew 11:29) and is where Paul got his theology of humility. This combination is also used in reference to being remade into the image of Jesus.

As you pursue peace and unity, as you love others, and as you consider others before yourself in humility and with gentleness, you are reflecting the life of Christ to the world. And in doing so, you are being remade into the image of Christ.

COMMIT

Take some time to read Acts 20:19, Philippians 2:3, Colossians 3:12, and 1 Peter 3:8. Meditate on these verses.

13

If, then, there is any encouragement in Christ, if any consolation of love, if any fellowship with the Spirit, if any affection and mercy, make my joy complete by thinking the same way, having the same love, united in spirit, intent on one purpose. Do nothing out of selfish ambition or conceit, but in humility consider others as more important than yourselves. Everyone should look not to his own interests, but rather to the interests of others.

—PHILIPPIANS 2:1–4

CONSIDER

Things start to fall apart when there is a lack of clarity in purpose. This is true for work environments, sports teams, and even families. Having a goal that everyone can get behind is crucial in getting people to move together and achieve something bigger than what they could on their own.

Paul posed his statement with a tone of possibility: "If, then, there is any encouragement in Christ . . ." Hearing this, everyone would have said, "Of course there is encouragement in Christ!"

Yes, this is the case, and it comes with an expectation. Exercising humility fosters joy, peace, and unity in the family of God.

CULTIVATE

It takes practice to consider others over yourself. It isn't a natural impulse of fallen humanity. However, it can be a trained impulse for followers of Jesus.

Considering others important doesn't mean you devalue yourself. In the same way Jesus willingly humbled himself in the incarnation, you are invited to bring humility into your relationships.

One of the ways to practice this is through the words you say about others in your mind. You can make it a practice to speak value, worth, and dignity about others as you interact with them.

COMMIT

Identify three people in your life with whom you want to practice considering their interests over your own.

For the next three days, when you see them or think about them, speak the truth of their value, worth, and dignity in your mind. Know this is an internal practice that will facilitate outward actions.

ACKNOWLEDGMENTS

TO MY MOM, dad, brother, and sister: thank you for teaching me the power of prayer, the power of family, and unconditional love. Mom, you've always lived your life with others in mind. It's been a powerful testimony of the other-centered life of Jesus. Thank you for all the sacrifices you made in life. I would never be who I am today without your love and support.

Ammamma and Thathaya (Grandma and Grandpa): your prayers have gone before me. You've lived a lifetime of humility, selflessly serving people in India who were on the margins and without hope. I will do my very best to follow you as you've faithfully followed Jesus all these years.

My extended family: what an honor to be raised by you. Thank you all (especially my mom's brothers and sisters and their spouses) for sacrificing years of your own lives to take care of me and raise me as a child. You truly are moms and dads to me, and I cherish the fact that I am a shared son among you all.

Britt: none of this would be possible without you. When I think of humble strength and confidence, I see you. As I wrote this book, you've been a silent strength in the background cheering

237

me on. You've sacrificed in heroic ways for me and our family. You believed I would be an author before I ever even entertained the thought. You are God's kindness and grace to me, and I am grateful every day for the family we have and the love we share.

Liam, Levi, Lucas, and EmJ: I pray that the words you read on these pages would be true of the life your dad lives (as imperfect as it may be). Thank you for showing me childlike humility and for being used by God to remind me of humility! You are my pride and joy.

Lysa TerKeurst: you have been a friend, mentor, and advocate for me around every turn. Learning from you is like watching MJ shoot a fadeaway. I could never thank you enough for your kindness and encouragement. Sitting under your Bible teaching has made me a better student of God's Word. Thank you, LT.

Meredith: you've been so much more than a literary agent for me. You've been a friend and you've championed this message from the very beginning. Thank you for never letting me settle and for believing in this vision of "humble theology" from the start.

Carrie: I knew from the beginning I needed a very specific type of editor. Well, you've been that and beyond. Thank you for believing in my words, fighting for the reader with every edit, and enduring my endless references to MJ, Chicago food, and sports! I'm so grateful for you and your attentive eye to detail and brilliance with words. Thank you for helping me sharpen and hone this message.

Damon: I still have the first message of encouragement you sent me on Instagram after the first time we met many years ago. After every COMPEL training I would tell the team, "I really like Damon. He's a theology nerd like me." Thank you for encouraging me before being an author was ever even a dream. And then when it did become a dream, thank you for making that dream come true. Having you as my publisher and being part of the W Team family of authors is such an honor.

Michael, Hope, Madi, Shae, Leah, Amanda: I learn so much from you all. You are brilliant with words, and you always remind me to do theology for the everyday average Bible reader. Thank you for always raising your hand, asking the best questions, and slowing me down.

Brittany T., Matt P., Megan, Alex and Mario, and J. Scott: I'm so indebted to you for your friendship, support, and encouragement along the way.

Chicago Boyz (you know who you are): you guys are my oldest and dearest friends. Y'all never let me drink my own Kool-Aid, you've kept me grounded, and I'm so grateful for that.

Proverbs 31 Ministries: what a joy to do life and ministry with you all. So grateful to be on this journey of "humble theology" with you as we work together to share the truth of God's Word.

Pastor Derwin and Transformation Church: thank you for creating an environment of humility within the family of God. And PD, I know you'll love the MJ references in the book. I thought of you each time I wrote them!

Uncle Scott (Logos Bible Software): I literally would not have been able to do the research for this book without Logos. Uncle Scott, thanks for all your help with training to help me become so much more efficient and effective in my theological research process.

The Heiniger family: Shara and the girls, thank you for allowing me to share Pete's (and your) story. I know Pete's story and your courage and bravery will bring hope and comfort to everyone who reads the chapter "When Bad Things Happen to Humble People."

NOTES

CHAPTER 1

1. John Gramlich, "Mental Health and the Pandemic: What U.S. Surveys Have Found," Pew Research Center, March 2, 2023, https://www.pewresearch.org /fact-tank/2023/03/02/mental-health-and-the-pandemic-what-u-s-surveys -have-found/.
2. "How Mental Health Is the New Domain of Ministry to the Next Generation," Barna, October 8, 2020, https://www.barna.com/research/mental-health-next-gen/.
3. Taylor Swift, vocalist, "Anti-Hero," by Taylor Swift and Jack Antonoff, track 3 on *Midnights*, Republic Records, 2022.

CHAPTER 2

1. Chad Brand et al., eds., s.v. "Archer," in *Holman Illustrated Bible Dictionary* (Nashville, TN: Holman Bible Publishers, 2003), 106. Elsewhere we find the phrase "breaking the bow," which was an equivalent to breaking the power of a person or nation (Hos. 1:5; Jer. 49:35). The Persian archers were some of the most feared and famous archers in the Ancient Near East (Isa. 13:18; Jer. 49:35; 50:9, 14, 29, 42).
2. Diether Kellermann, "הִלְגֵּעַ," in *Theological Dictionary of the Old Testament*, ed. G. Johannes Botterweck, Helmer Ringgren, and Heinz-Josef Fabry, trans. David E. Green and Douglas W. Stott (Grand Rapids, MI: William B. Eerdmans, 1999), 453.
3. John Gill, *Gill's Exposition of the Entire Bible* [1746–63], Psalm 46:9, available at BibleHub, https://biblehub.com/commentaries/psalms/46-9.htm.

CHAPTER 3

1. Years later I was watching an episode of *The Walking Dead* and realized that my favorite character in the show, Daryl, found a dog and named him Dog, so I think I'm in good company now.

2. David G. Peterson, *The Acts of the Apostles*, The Pillar New Testament Commentary (Grand Rapids, MI: William B. Eerdmans, 2009), 498.
3. Ben Witherington refers to the usage in nonbiblical Greek literature, such as Aristophanes, *Ec.*, line 315; *Pax*, 691; and Plato, *Phaedo*, 99b. See Ben Witherington III, *The Acts of the Apostles: A Socio-Rhetorical Commentary* (Grand Rapids, MI: William B. Eerdmans, 1998), 528. Additionally, the word is used in the Septuagint in reference to blindness and darkness. See Isa. 59:10; Judg. 16:26; Deut. 28:29; Job 5:13–14, 12:25.

CHAPTER 4

1. Teresa of Ávila, *Minor Works of St. Teresa*, trans. Benedictines of Stanbrook (London: Thomas Baker, 1913), 154.
2. John Dickson, *Humilitas: A Lost Key to Life, Love, and Leadership* (Grand Rapids, MI: Zondervan, 2011), 127.
3. J. I. Packer, *Weakness Is the Way: Life with Christ Our Strength* (Wheaton, IL: Crossway, 2013).
4. Nahum M. Sarna, *Genesis*, vol. 1 of *The JPS Torah Commentary* (Philadelphia: Jewish Publication Society, 1989), 12.
5. Stephen G. Dempster, *Dominion and Dynasty: A Biblical Theology of the Hebrew Bible*, vol. 15 of *New Studies in Biblical Theology*, ed. D.A. Carson (Downers Grove, IL: InterVarsity Press, 2003), 59.
6. Saint Augustine, *Confessions*, trans. Vernon J. Bourke, vol. 21 of *The Fathers of the Church*, ed. Roy Joseph Deferrari (Washington, DC: The Catholic University of America Press, 1953), 329.

CHAPTER 5

1. Timothy G. Gombis, *Power in Weakness: Paul's Transformed Vision for Ministry* (Grand Rapids, MI: William B. Eerdmans, 2021), 21.

CHAPTER 6

1. Thomas à Kempis, *Humility and the Elevation of the Mind to God*, trans. Robert Nixon (Gastonia, NC: TAN Books), 2021, 4.
2. Ann Voskamp and Darryl Stolt (interview, session 1, IF:Gathering, Dallas, TX, March 3, 2023).
3. Jim Cress, email message to author, April 5, 2023; Alison Cook, email message to author, March 7, 2023.
4. William Lee Holladay, e.d., *A Concise Hebrew and Aramaic Lexicon of the Old Testament* (Leiden, NL: Brill, 2000), 171.
5. Dietrich von Hildebrand, *Humility: Wellspring of Virtue* (Manchester, NH: Sophia Institute Press, 1997), 6.
6. Diether Kellermann, s.v. "הָאַג," in *Theological Dictionary of the Old Testament*, ed. G. Johannes Botterweck and Helmer Ringgren, trans. John T. Willis (Grand Rapids, MI: William B. Eerdmans, 1977), 345.
7. Ludwig Koehler et al., *The Hebrew and Aramaic Lexicon of the Old Testament* (Leiden, NL: Brill, 1994–2000), 169.

NOTES

8. Jürgen Blunck, s.v. *"Ὕψος,"* in *New International Dictionary of New Testament Theology,* ed. Colin Brown (Grand Rapids, MI: Regency Reference Library, 1976), 199. The Greek translation of the Hebrew Old Testament is called the Septuagint. We could even consider the Septuagint one of the earliest commentaries of the Old Testament Hebrew Bible.

9. Blunck, *"Ὕψος,"* 199.

10. William Whitaker, *Dictionary of Latin Forms* (Bellingham, WA: Logos Bible Software, 2012). The Latin form *humus* is used in the vulgate for the ground in Genesis 2:9, 19.

11. Richard J. Foster, *Learning Humility: A Year of Searching for a Vanishing Virtue* (Downers Grove, IL: InterVarsity Press, 2022), 9–10.

CHAPTER 7

1. Alexa Carlton, "Why Are Cats So Curious: Science Explains This Feline Trait," Traveling With Your Cat, May 30, 2021, https://www.travelingwithyourcat.com /why-are-cats-so-curious/. If you want to watch some cats being curious, check out "Curious Cats," YouTube, posted by DailyPicksandFlicks, January 24, 2018, https://www.youtube.com/watch?v=eKjAMCcIgPY.

2. Michael S. Heiser, *The Unseen Realm: Recovering the Supernatural Worldview of the Bible* (Bellingham, WA: Lexham Press, 2015), 87–90. See also Marcus Jastrow, *A Dictionary of the Targumim, the Talmud Babli and Yerushalmi, and the Midrashic Literature,* vol. 1 and 2 (New York: G. P. Putnam's Sons, 1903), 896 (ðçùÑ II); and Jacob Hoftijzer et al., *Dictionary of the North-West Semitic Inscriptions,* 2 vols. (Leiden, NL: Brill, 1995), 2.726 (nḥš6).

3. Heiser, *The Unseen Realm,* 88.

4. The prophet Ezekiel did something really intriguing in these verses. He used a human king (the king of Tyre) as an entry point to explain a supernatural situation, the fall of Satan. Here is the full text of the passage I'm referring to in this discussion:

> "Son of man, lament for the king of Tyre and say to him, 'This is what the LORD God says: You were the seal of perfection, full of wisdom and perfect in beauty. You were in Eden, the garden of God. Every kind of precious stone covered you: carnelian, topaz, and diamond, beryl, onyx, and jasper, lapis lazuli, turquoise and emerald. Your mountings and settings were crafted in gold; they were prepared on the day you were created.
>
> 'You were an anointed guardian cherub, for I had appointed you. You were on the holy mountain of God; you walked among the fiery stones. From the day you were created you were blameless in your ways until wickedness was found in you.
>
> 'Through the abundance of your trade, you were filled with violence, and you sinned. So I expelled you in disgrace from the mountain of God, and banished you, guardian cherub, from among the fiery stones. Your heart became proud because of your beauty; For the sake of your splendor you corrupted your wisdom.

So I threw you down to the ground; I made you a spectacle before kings'" (Ezek. 28:12–17).

5. Isaiah employed the same literary strategy as Ezekiel. There is a reference to a human king, but the narrative speaks to a supernatural event. Namely, the fall of Satan.

6. Origen, *The Philocalia of Origen*, trans. George Lewis (Edinburgh: T&T Clark, 1911), 149.

7. J. N. Bremmer, s.v. "Narcissus," in *Dictionary of Deities and Demons in the Bible*, 2nd ed., ed. Karel van der Toorn, Bob Becking, and Pieter W. van der Horst (Grand Rapids, MI: William B. Eerdmans, 1999), 614.

8. The scriptural accounts of Satan date back to the sixth (Ezekiel) and eighth (Isaiah) centuries BC, while the myth of Narcissus likely emerged in the early AD first century. "Book of Ezekiel," NIV Study Bible, Zondervan, 2002, Bible Study Tools, https://www.biblestudytools.com/ezekiel/; "Who Wrote the Book of Isaiah?" *Zondervan Academic* (blog), December 6, 2018, https://zondervanacademic.com/blog/who-wrote-isaiah; Kimberly Lin, "Narcissus Myth: Early Poets and the Ancient Story," Historic Mysteries, January 7, 2018, https://www.historicmysteries.com/narcissus-myth-version -poets/.

9. Lysa TerKeurst, Jim Cress, and Joel Muddamalle, "Narcissism . . . What It Is and What It Isn't," August 29, 2022, in *Therapy & Theology* podcast, Season 1, Episode 6, https://www.iheart.com/podcast/867-therapy-and-theology-101789380/episode /s1-e6-narcissism-what-101789464/.

10. Franco Montanari, Madeleine Goh, and Chad Schroeder, ed., *The Brill Dictionary of Ancient Greek* (Leiden, NL: Brill, 2015), accessed via Logos Digital Software.

11. Lysa TerKeurst, *Unglued: Making Wise Choices in the Midst of Raw Emotions* (Nashville, TN: Thomas Nelson, 2012), 72.

12. Bernard of Clairvaux, *Treatises II: The Steps of Humility and Pride*, (Collegeville, MN: Liturgical Press, 1989), 42.

13. Heiser, *The Unseen Realm*, 91.

14. The same idea is present earlier in James 1:9.

CHAPTER 8

1. Jared Dubin, "Former Raiders WR Henry Ruggs III Pleads Guilty to Two Charges Stemming from Fatal DUI Crash," CBS Sports, May 10, 2023, https:// www.cbssports.com/nfl/news/former-raiders-wr-henry-ruggs-iii-pleads-guilty-to -two-charges-stemming-from-fatal-dui-crash/.

2. Georgie Kearney, "Will Smith Oscars Slap: Actor Blames 'Bottled Rage' As Reason Why He 'Lost It,'" 7Life, 7 News.com.au, November 29, 2022, https://7news .com.au/entertainment/celebrity/will-smith-oscars-slap-actor-blames-bottled-rage -as-reason-why-he-lost-it-c-9010057.

3. "A Statement from the Willis Family," The Association for Frontotemporal Degeneration, February 16, 2023, https://www.theaftd.org/mnlstatement23/.

4. Zendaya (@zendayalatest), "Just had the worst panic attack . . ." posted October 9, 2020, https://www.instagram.com/p/CGGZBNcDNq5/?hl=en.

NOTES

5. Lauren Russell, "Zendaya Health: 'I Don't Have It Under Control Yet'—Actress on 'The Key' to Help Anxiety," *Express*, March 4, 2022, https://www.express .co.uk/life-style/health/1575530/zendaya-health-anxiety-symptoms-treatment -therapy.
6. As quoted in Richard J. Foster, *Learning Humility: A Year of Searching for a Vanishing Virtue* (Downers Grove: InterVarsity Press, 2022), 12.
7. J. G. Plöger, "הֲמָדָא," in *Theological Dictionary of the Old Testament*, ed. G. Johannes Botterweck and Helmer Ringgren, trans. John T. Willis (Grand Rapids, MI: William B. Eerdmans, 1977), 88. The related Akkadian term *adamātu* means "dark, red soil," showing how these words related to each other conceptually in the Ancient Near Eastern world.
8. G. K. Chesterton, *Heretics* (New York: John Lane, 1905), 87.
9. Eugene H. Peterson, *The Contemplative Pastor: Returning to the Art of Spiritual Direction*, vol. 17, *The Leadership Library* (Carol Stream, IL; Dallas; Waco, TX: Christianity Today, 1989), 122.

CHAPTER 9

1. Here are a few examples:

"There is no Christianity without humility, which is the foundation of all improvement, and the soil, in which faith in Christ, is planted." John Burns, *The Principles of Christian Philosophy: Containing the Doctrines, Duties, Admonitions, and Consolations of the Christian Religion* (Philadephia, PA: Carey, 1833), 150.

"[Humility] is the blessed soil out of which all graces grow." Rev. T. T. Carter, quoted in Edwin Davies, *Select Thoughts on Ministry and the Church* (London: William Tegg and Co., 1875), 288.

"Supposing the soil to be good, it grows well and bears much fruit, with thyself. Are they roots, that is to say, thy intentions, not planted in the good, fertile soil that God alone is, in real and submissive humility?" John Tauler, *The Sermons and Conferences of John Tauler of the Order of Preachers* (Washington, DC: Apostolic Mission House, 1910), 83.

"Only on the soil of true humility can genuine Christian virtue grow." Benedict Baur, *Silence with God* (Washington, DC: Henry Regnery Co., 1955), 119.

2. Andrew Murray, *Humility: The Journey Toward Holiness* (Minneapolis: Bethany House, 2001), 17.
3. Murray, *Humility*, 17.
4. Herbert W. Basser, s.v. "Priests and Priesthood, Jewish," in *Dictionary of New Testament Background: A Compendium of Contemporary Biblical Scholarship*, ed. Craig A. Evans and Stanley E. Porter (Downers Grove, IL: InterVarsity

Press, 2000), 825; Charles Meeks, s.v. "Priesthood," *The Lexham Bible Dictionary*, ed. John D. Barry et al. (Bellingham, WA: Lexham Press, 2016).

5. This breakdown of four parts can be found in the *Lexham Context Commentary*, 8 vols., ed. Douglas Mangum and Steven E. Runge (Bellingham, WA: Lexham Press, 2020). These four parts are an adaptation from that list.

CHAPTER 10

1. References to "the way" are found in Acts 9:2; 19:9, 23; 22:4; 24:14, 22. Tomas Bokedal, s.v. "The Way," in *The Lexham Bible Dictionary*, ed. John D. Barry, et al. (Bellingham, WA: Lexham Press, 2016).

2. Leon Morris, *The Gospel According to Matthew*, The Pillar New Testament Commentary (Grand Rapids, MI: William B. Eerdmans, 1992), 296.

3. New Testament scholars are divided on whether the yoke in view here is a human yoke or animal yoke. I tend to believe that both can be in view but the metaphor /image should not be taken further than the text allows.

4. Morris, *The Gospel According to Matthew*, 296.

5. Grant R. Osborne, *Matthew*, vol. 1 of *Zondervan: Exegetical Commentary on the New Testament*, ed. Clinton E. Arnold (Grand Rapids, MI: Zondervan, 2010), 443.

6. Andrew Murray, *Humility: The Journey Toward Holiness* (Minneapolis, MN: Bethany House, 2001), 25.

7. Katherine Sonderegger, *Systematic Theology: Volume 1; The Doctrine of God* (Minneapolis: Fortress, 2015), 151–332.

8. The concept of "divine humility" is mentioned by Augustine, who said, "Moreover, the one cleansing of sinful and proud men is the blood of the Just One and the humbling of God. For in order to contemplate God, which we are not by nature, we had to be cleansed through Him, who became what we are by nature, and what we are not by sin." See St. Augustine, *The Trinity*, ed. Hermigild Dressler, trans. Stephen McKenna, vol. 45, *The Fathers of the Church* (Washington, DC: The Catholic University of America Press, 1963), 133; R. S. Anderson, s.v. "Son of God," in *The International Standard Bible Encyclopedia, Revised*, ed. Geoffrey W. Bromiley (Grand Rapids, MI: William B. Eerdmans, 1979–1988), 573.

9. This content was inspired by a sermon from Michael Ramsey, Archbishop of Canterbury. He was discussing the importance of humility to a group of people who were preparing to be ordained for ministry. The list here is an adaptation of his bullet points. I came across this material first in John Stott, *The Radical Disciple: Some Neglected Aspects of Our Calling* (Downers Grove, IL: IVP Books, 2010).

10. Michael J. Gorman, *Cruciformity: Paul's Narrative Spirituality of the Cross* (Grand Rapids, MI: William B. Eerdmans, 2001).

CHAPTER 11

1. Walter Grundmann, s.v. "Ταπεινός, Ταπεινόω, Ταπείνωσις, Ταπεινόφρων, Ταπεινοφροσύνη," in *Theological Dictionary of the New Testament* ed. Gerhard Kittel, Geoffrey W. Bromiley, and Gerhard Friedrich (Grand Rapids, MI: William B. Eerdmans, 1964), 11–12.

NOTES

2. Markus Barth and Helmut Blanke, eds., and Astrid B. Beck, trans., *Colossians: A New Translation with Introduction and Commentary*, vol. 34B of *The Anchor Yale Bible*, ed. John J. Collins (New Haven: Yale University Press, 2008), 343.
3. H. H. Esser, s.v. "Ταπεινός," in *New International Dictionary of New Testament Theology*, ed. Colin Brown (Grand Rapids, MI: Zondervan, 1976), 260. A point of nuance: This is not to say that any form of modesty was absent in the Greco-Roman world or that the concept of "humility" was negative without exception. Of course there were exceptions, but they were infrequent and not normative. In other words, humility was not viewed as a virtue in the Greco-Roman world. Paul radically changed this concept when he connected it to what is possibly the most important virtue of the Christian life.
4. John H. Elliott, *1 Peter: A New Translation with Introduction and Commentary*, vol. 37B of *The Anchor Yale Bible*, ed. John J. Collins (New Haven: Yale University Press, 2008), 605.
5. Saint Augustine, *Confessions*, trans. Vernon J. Bourke, vol. 21 of *The Fathers of the Church* (Washington, DC: The Catholic University of America Press, 1953), 714.
6. Eve-Marie Becker, *Paul on Humility*, trans. Wayne Coppins (Waco, TX: Baylor University Press, 2020), 1.
7. Becker, *Paul on Humility*, 53.
8. Jonathan N. Cleland, s.v. "Monasticism," in *The Essential Lexham Dictionary of Church History*, ed. Michael A. G. Haykin (Bellingham, WA: Lexham Press, 2022).
9. Becker, *Paul on Humility*, 29.
10. Adam Webb, "Harnessing the Power of Your Reality Distortion Field," *Forbes,* October 4, 2021, https://www.forbes.com/sites/forbesbusinessdevelopmentcouncil /2021/10/04/harnessing-the-power-of-your-reality-distortion-field /?sh=7e024d3e6f9f.

CHAPTER 12

1. Lauren Bedosky, "5 Possible Health Benefits of Cold Water Therapy," Everyday Health, December 12, 2022, https://www.everydayhealth.com/wellness/possible -health-benefits-to-cold-water-therapy/.
2. Arne Öhman, "The Role of the Amygdala in Human Fear: Automatic Detection of Threat," *Psychoneuroendocrinology* 30, no. 10 (November 2005): 953–58, https:// doi.org/10.1016/j.psyneuen.2005.03.019.
3. *American Psychological Association Dictionary of Psychology*, s.v. "fear," accessed May 31, 2023, https://dictionary.apa.org/fear.
4. "Understanding the Stress Response," Harvard Health Publishing, Harvard Medical School, July 6, 2020, https://www.health.harvard.edu/staying-healthy /understanding-the-stress-response.

CHAPTER 13

1. Check out the *Daily Show* episode where comedian Hasan Minhaj brings light to this in a funny but very true way! *The Daily Show*, Season 28, Episode 55 at 9 minutes into the show. You're welcome.

NOTES

2. Gene L. Green, *The Letters to the Thessalonians*, The Pillar New Testament Commentary (Grand Rapids, MI; Leicester, England: William B. Eerdmans; Apollos, 2002), 203.

CHAPTER 14

1. Gerhard Friedrich, s.v. "Εὐαγγελίζομαι, Εὐαγγέλιον, Προευαγγελίζομαι, Εὐαγγελιστής," in *Theological Dictionary of the New Testament*, ed. Gerhard Kittel, Geoffrey W. Bromiley, and Gerhard Friedrich (Grand Rapids, MI: William B. Eerdmans, 1964), 707.

2. Some may question the humility of God the Father, but we do find the concept of humility connected to him in Scripture. The very act of swooping low to breathe the breath of life into humans, who were made from dust, was an act of humility in the opening pages of Genesis. God gives us what we do not deserve and what only he has a right to.

   Orthodox teaching holds that the Trinitarian Godhead shares one divine nature; ontologically (in their "being"), they are one. In my view, to say the Son is exclusively humble and the Father is not is a contradiction.

   In addition to attaching the image and concept of humility to God the Father, Scripture gives us a lexical connection. For example, Psalm 113:5–8 says, "Who is like the LORD our God—the one enthroned on high, who *stoops* down to look on the heavens and the earth? He raises the poor from the dust and lifts the needy from the trash heap in order to seat them with nobles—with the nobles of his people."

   The word *stoops* in the CSB here is translated from the Hebrew word *sapel*, which means to "be humble" or "to bow low." The Septuagint translates that Hebrew word, *sapel*, into Greek as *tapeina*, meaning "humble."

   And so, this text displays God the Father being "humble" in a manner unique to God.

   For further discussion of divine humility, see Katherine Sonderegger, *Systematic Theology: Volume 1; The Doctrine of God*, (Minneapolis: Fortress, 2015), 151–332.

3. G. K. Beale, *The Temple and the Church's Mission: A Biblical Theology of the Dwelling Place of God*, vol. 17 of *New Studies in Biblical Theology*, ed. D. A. Carson, (Downers Grove, IL: IVP Academic, 2004), 30. Beale goes on to say, "The divine provision of clothing to Adam and Eve in Genesis 3:21 appears to indicate a gracious reaffirmation of their inheritance rights over creation, despite their former rebellion."

4. Jim Cress, Lysa TerKeurst, and Joel Muddamalle, "Good Boundaries Lead to Better Relationships," August 29, 2022, in *Therapy & Theology* podcast, Season 1, Episode 8, https://therapyandtheology.transistor.fm/episodes/good-boundaries -lead-to-better-relationships/transcript.

5. F. J. Stendebach, s.v. "עוֹלָם," in *Theological Dictionary of the Old Testament*, ed. G. Johannes Botterweck, Helmer Ringgren, and Heinz-Josef Fabry, trans. David E. Green (Grand Rapids, MI: William B. Eerdmans, 2006), 18.

6. William Sinclair, "Humility," *The Churchman* 12, no. 4–11 (1898), 319.

NOTES

CHAPTER 15

1. Faith Karimi, "A Man Strangled a Chicago Student After She Wouldn't Talk to Him, Prosecutors Say," CNN, November 27, 2019, https://www.cnn.com/2019/11/27/us/university-of-illinois-chicago-ruth-george/index.html.

2. Stephen R. Haynes and Lori Brandt Hale, *Bonhoeffer for Armchair Theologians*, Armchair Theologians Series (Louisville, KY: Westminster John Knox, 2009), 148–149.

3. S. Payne, *The Venlo Incident* (London: Hutchinson, 1950), 180.

4. Ferdinand Schlingensiepen, *Dietrich Bonhoeffer 1906–1945: Martyr, Thinker, Man of Resistance*, trans. Isabel Best (London: T&T Clark, 2012), 375.

5. Schlingensiepen, *Dietrich Bonhoeffer 1906–1945*, 378.

6. Dietrich Bonhoeffer, *The Cost of Discipleship* (London: SCM Press, 2015) 47.

7. Dietrich Bonhoeffer, *The Communion of Saints* (New York: Harper & Row, 1964), 20.

8. Marvin H. Pope, *Job: Introduction, Translation, and Notes*, vol. 15 of *The Anchor Yale Bible* (New Haven: Yale University Press, 1965), 9.

9. David J. A. Clines, *Job 1–20*, vol. 17 of the *Word Biblical Commentary* (Dallas: Word, Incorporated, 1989), 24.

10. Craig G. Bartholomew, "Hearing the Old Testament Wisdom Literature: The Wit of Many and the Wisdom of One," in *Hearing the Old Testament: Listening for God's Address*, ed. Craig G. Bartholomew and David J. H. Beldman (Grand Rapids, MI: William B. Eerdmans, 2012), 317.

11. Eric Ortlund, *Piercing Leviathan: God's Defeat of Evil in the Book of Job*, vol. 56 of *New Studies in Biblical Theology*, ed. D. A. Carson, (London; Downers Grove, IL: Apollos; IVP Academic, 2021), 69.

12. Ortlund, *Piercing Leviathan*, 69.

13. Michael V. Fox, "Job 38 and God's Rhetoric," in *Semeia*, ed. John Dominic Crossan, 19 (1981), 58.

CONCLUSION

1. John Blanchard, *The Complete Gathered Gold: A Treasury of Quotations for Christians* (Welwyn Garden City, UK: Evangelical Press, 2006).

2. John R. W. Stott, "Pride, Humility and God," C. S. Lewis Institute, *Sovereign Grace Magazine*, September/October 2000, http://www.cslewisinstitute.org/webfm_send/375.

3. Martin Luther is credited with this concept, but he most likely got it from Augustine. Luther referred to it in Latin as *homo incurvatus in se*, or "man turned in on himself." Eberhard Jüngel, *Justification: The Heart of the Christian Faith* (Edinburgh: T&T Clark, 2001), 145. See also St. Augustine, *The City of God, Books VIII–XVI*, ed. Hermigild Dressler, trans. Gerald G. Walsh and Grace Monahan, vol. 14 of *The Fathers of the Church* (Washington, DC: The Catholic University of America Press, 1952), 476.

4. "Peterson: In Between the Man and the Message," YouTube, posted by NavPress, August 31, 2016, https://youtu.be/LaMgIvbXqSk, time stamp: 5:40.

5. Teresa of Ávila, *Interior Castle*, trans. E. Allison Peers, (Mineola, NY: Dover Publications, 2007), 11.

6. Johannes P. Louw and Eugene Albert Nida, *Greek-English Lexicon of the New Testament: Based on Semantic Domains* (New York: United Bible Societies, 1996), 481.
7. Murray J. Harris, *The Second Epistle to the Corinthians: A Commentary on the Greek Text*, The New International Greek Testament Commentary (Grand Rapids, MI; Milton Keynes, UK: William B. Eerdmans; Paternoster Press, 2005), 445–446.

APPENDIX

1. Derek Kidner, *Proverbs: An Introduction and Commentary*, vol. 17 of the *Tyndale Old Testament Commentaries*, ed. D. J. Wiseman (Downers Grove, IL: InterVarsity Press, 1964), 113.
2. I heard this on the show *First Take* and I believe it was Stephen A. Smith who first said it. This was in reference to chronic traumatic encephalopathy (CTE) and football.
3. Bruce K. Waltke, *The Book of Proverbs: Chapters 15–31*, The New International Commentary on the Old Testament (Grand Rapids, MI: William B. Eerdmans, 2005), 76.

ABOUT THE AUTHOR

HOLDING A PHD in theology, Joel Muddamalle is the director of theology and research at Proverbs 31 Ministries with Lysa TerKeurst and the theologian in residence for Haven Place Ministries, a ministry of Lysa's that provides personalized theology and therapy retreats and smaller gatherings. He also cohosts the popular podcast *Therapy & Theology* with Lysa TerKeurst and licensed counselor Jim Cress.

Joel serves on the preaching team at Transformation Church with Pastor Derwin Gray and is a frequent speaker for conferences and events (She Speaks, IF:Gathering, Q Ideas NXT Gen Summit, Hope Heals Camp). One of his favorite things to do is lead in-depth theology workshops and training seminars for churches (Fresh Life, Passion City, Transformation Church).

Joel coauthored *30 Days with Jesus: Experiencing His Presence Throughout the Old and New Testaments* and has had the honor of working with Christian authors (Christine Caine, Jennie Allen, Bianca Olthoff, Jeff Bethke, Jon Tyson, Levi Lusko) consulting on the theological framework of their books through COMPEL consulting.

Based in Charlotte, North Carolina, Joel and his wife enjoy a full house with their four children and two dogs. If he doesn't have a theology book in his hand, you can be sure he's either coaching one of his kids in a sport, getting roped into a reel by his wife (@ almostindianwife), or doing his best to keep up his hoops game on the basketball court on Tuesday nights with the guys—then going for a cold plunge. Yeah, it's a thing.

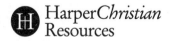

THE PROVERBS 31 MINISTRIES

Podcast Network

THE TRUTH YOU NEED TO NAVIGATE A WORLD FULL OF NOISE.

Welcome to The Proverbs 31 Ministries Podcast Network!
We've curated a family of shows that will help you know the Truth
and live the Truth because when you do, it changes everything.

CHECK OUT OUR SHOWS WHEREVER
YOU LISTEN TO YOUR PODCASTS:

The Proverbs 31 Ministries Podcast.
Encouragement for Today Podcast.
Therapy & Theology with Lysa TerKeurst
and Dr. Joel Muddamalle.

ALSO AVAILABLE WHEREVER BOOKS ARE SOLD.

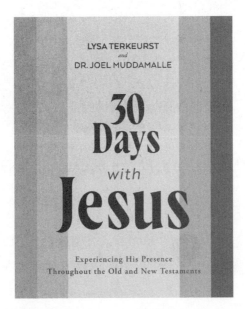